# Freedom and Faith

# Freedom and Faith

## *A Question of Scottish Identity*

Donald Smith

SAINT ANDREW PRESS
Edinburgh

First published in 2013 by
SAINT ANDREW PRESS
121 George Street
Edinburgh EH2 4YN

ISBN 978-0-86153-813-3

The opinions expressed in this book are those of the author and do not
necessarily reflect those of the publisher.

British Library Cataloguing in Publication Data
A catalogue record for this book is available from the British Library.

Scripture quotations taken from the
HOLY BIBLE, NEW INTERNATIONAL VERSION.
Copyright © 1973, 1978, 1984 by International Bible Society

It is the publisher's policy to only use papers that are natural and recyclable
and that have been manufactured from timber grown in renewable, properly
managed forests. All of the manufacturing processes of the papers are expected
to conform to the environmental regulations of the country of origin.

Typeset by Manila Typesetting Company
Printed and bound in the United Kingdom by
Ashford Colour Press Ltd., Gosport, Hampshire.

# Contents

# In Memoriam

## ARCHIE CRAIG (1888–1985)

### *Faith and Life*

'For we build citadels around our lives against each other, hoping thus to find security, and fearing lest fellowship should rob us of our freedom. So we blaspheme you with our lives, even while we bless you with our lips, and run upon death, mistaking it for life and bliss.'    *Broadcast prayer*

# Foreword

## HARRY REID

In this short book Donald Smith has achieved the well-nigh miraculous.

With both fair-mindedness and finesse, he explains the course of Scotland's long and often problematic relationship with Christianity. Sometimes wracked by violent and vicious division, but just as frequently marked by numinous and far-sighted aspiration, the narratives and challenges of Scotland's Christian life have been complex. Somehow Donald Smith manages to steer a calm and reflective course through this mixture of grace and turbulence.

He discusses and analyses a small but complicated nation's Christianity with lucid authority and good sense. Towards the end, he changes tack and preaches just a little, but in a gentle rather than hectoring way. This adds to the rich texture of this remarkable book which is at once deeply personal and magnanimously objective.

Indeed Donald Smith comes close to presenting a manifesto for a better Scotland, although I'm sure he is too modest to put it quite like that. He certainly provides a refreshing, perceptive and above all Christian perspective on Scotland's ongoing political and constitutional conundrums.

As an author and journalist who has over many years grappled with the issues discussed in this fine book, I read Donald's reflections with fascination. And as I am also a Scot – we are a very disputatious people – it's pretty well inevitable that I should disagree with some of the points he makes, and indeed with some of his graciously reached conclusions. Yet in no way does that inhibit me from heaping lavish praise on his book.

Indeed it is because I have engaged with many of the debates and controversies that he covers that I believe I can commend his book with real enthusiasm.

The pages that follow are full of freshness. There is a keen sense of clean air blowing through them. The book totally lacks stuffiness. It will fascinate, enlighten and encourage anyone currently engaged in Christian life and work in Scotland – and there are hundreds of thousands of us. In addition, these pages may also serve as a kind of handbook to outsiders who at this special and significant time may be seeking some understanding of the nature of Scotland and its ongoing journey. To use an old fashioned but valuable word, this book is all about Scotland's quiddity

Many Scots are currently contending for their nation's independence; many others are resisting this movement. In this particular context it is most useful to have such a careful and considered exploration of many of the key aspects and components of Scotland's national identity, and especially its religious identity.

This is a time when many Scots, and so many others too, are trying to work out how Scotland has arrived at this pivotal point in its long and erratic journey. In this context, I expect that Donald Smith's book will prove exceptionally useful. It has every right to acquire the status of an especially insightful Christian guide to Scotland's past, present and future.

# Introduction

## *Starting Point*

It is September 2012 and I am back in the Martin Hall at New College, Edinburgh University's Divinity Faculty, after a gap of 33 years.

The occasion is the launch of *Arguing for Independence*, Stephen Maxwell's final, posthumously published work, devoted to a cause for which he expended a lifetime of thinking and action. Stephen's son Jamie is speaking along with Alex Salmond, First Minister of Scotland, Jim Eadie and Joyce McMillan, and the ebullient Owen Dudley Edwards is the host on behalf of Luath Publishing.

It seems an unusual choice of venue, but resonant for me. In 1979 when I left New College to go to the School of Scottish Studies, Stephen Maxwell was an influence around the university and city, championing a radical agenda for nationalism and an internationalist engagement with world development. Also by June 1979 the depressingly inconclusive Devolution Referendum had just taken place in Scotland. The immediate aftermath was downbeat, and might have been worse had we known what was about to come, setting back Scottish politics for another 20 years. I remember attending a rather sombre final Communion service here in the Martin Hall and wondering what the future might hold, while also feeling that mine lay elsewhere.

Matters religious were not, however, on the agenda at this packed occasion in 2012. Stephen Maxwell's characteristically rigorous mind tackles the democratic, economic, social, international, cultural and environmental cases for Scottish independence. In each case he considers evidence, risk and what he calls 'the wicked issues' which address some familiar and much used arguments against Scottish nationalism. Alex Salmond speaks particularly well, with affectionate humility, in tribute to the strategic thinking, debating skills and steadiness of an old friend and political comrade. In the aftermath of the 1979 Referendum failure both men were expelled for a time from the Scottish National Party (SNP). How things change.

In his final remarks, Owen Dudley Edwards refers to the venue and to the moral and spiritual aspects of the independence question, including the Trident nuclear missiles housed on the Clyde. That makes explicit what is implicit at several points in *Arguing for Independence*. The 'cultural case' in Maxwell's treatment for example deals directly with moral freedoms and responsibilities in relation to cultural autonomy. None the less, religion is not directly considered as contributing to arguments for or against. Stephen Maxwell chose not to do this, though one of the 'wicked issues' he fields is the canard that in an independent Scotland the forces of sectarianism would be released to wreck havoc as never before.

What are the religious implications of Scotland's rediscovered statehood, and of the choices that are now presented for the future? Considering my own experience, I can see that religion has been bound up with my social existence for good and ill since the cradle. Born in Glasgow in the care of a Church of Scotland residential home, I was adopted into a manse family and brought up with a dual Church and community inheritance. In 1956 when my personal journey began, over three million people in Scotland were associated with the National Kirk, while other traditions – including the Roman Catholic Church in Scotland – enjoyed high levels of active participation. Later my church experience was to branch out into an ecumenical meeting of traditions and faiths.

Political choice cannot be isolated from such experiences. And the rapid changes in religion in Scotland since the 1970s must have affected political developments in a variety of ways. In 1956 it would have been inconceivable to suggest a separation of politics and religion in Scotland, whereas now that seems a credible question to consider. Where does such dramatic change leave the moral dimension of politics and the political dimension of spirituality?

This book began to take shape in my mind that evening. One of my good fortunes as Director of the Scottish Storytelling Centre has been to move across many networks – political, cultural, religious, communitarian and environmental – listening to what people are saying now about Scotland as a country and society. I hope I have done more hearing than talking – though I confess to some of the verbal stuff as well. The art of storytelling has taught me how you have to listen attentively for the mind and spirit within the voice, beyond the words.

For all those who have spoken and listened I give my grateful thanks. And especially I pay my own tribute to Stephen Maxwell for the lucid clarity and stimulus which set me on a course of radical questions. For the outcome, though, I have only myself to blame.

Donald Smith
July 2012

# I

# The State We Are In

From 1707 to 1997 Scotland was a stateless nation. Though it had many of the normal expressions of nationhood, including a monarchy, a separate legal system, a national Church and a distinctive system of education, there was no Scottish government. Instead Scotland had united its national parliament with that of England and Wales at Westminster in London.

Likewise, the administrative or executive side of government was united in London. In 1800 Ireland was added to this shared entity, following the failed uprising of 1798. In the late twentieth century both Scotland and Ireland – or at least the remaining six British counties of Northern Ireland – both regained a degree of self-government through the devolution of powers from the UK.

Scottish constitutionalists have maintained that the union between Scotland and England enacted in 1707 is a partnership of equal nations. This was never more than a theory, since realistically the united parliament has been dominated by English representation. Aspects of Scotland's remaining constitutional independence, such as its religious settlement, were soon brought into question by the Westminster Parliament. Moreover, within a year of the 1707 union, nationalist resistance was taking a military form through the Jacobite movement.

In more recent times, it was made clear to Scots in 2013 that were they to vote for independence in 2014, they would be leaving, and not dissolving, the UK. This position was reinforced by the EU, whose larger member states have no wish to encourage movements for national independence within their own borders. So despite the specific legal position of Scotland as a continuing nation within the UK, *realpolitik* demanded that Scotland would have to apply for membership of the EU. The rest of the dissolved union would by contrast automatically continue in membership.

Why did Scotland become a stateless nation? And why, having entered into that condition, did Scotland not fully assimilate into Great Britain? The answers to these questions have major social, cultural and economic implications. Taken together they explain Scotland as it is today, and the nature of the choices that lie before its citizens.

Like all nations, Scotland is an invented concept. There is nothing inevitable or natural about it, and at various junctures the territory that is known as Scotland might have been part of England, Norway or Ireland.

The early history of what we now call Scotland was in reality a tug of war between different geographical spheres of influence. The first settlers came after the Ice Age from the European mainland, at a time when the British Isles were still physically joined to Europe. That land bridge was submerged as the sea waters rose. Later people also moved between Scotland and Ireland, and finally in the era of written history raiders turned settlers came from Scandinavia.

By the time the Romans had tried to conquer Scotland but settled instead for frontier walls, there were three related yet distinct cultural groupings. South of the Forth–Clyde line there were British Celtic or Brythonic peoples who spoke a P Celtic language akin to later Welsh. They were closely related to the kin-based culture encountered by the Romans in Britain as a whole. To the west, concentrated in Argyll, people speaking a Q Celtic language akin to later Gaelic and Irish were dominant, and in close cultural contact with Ireland. North of the Forth–Clyde line people now known as Picts were established, probably speaking a P Celtic language that has not survived. It is possible that some people of Germanic origin were already established on the east side of Scotland within these Celtic groupings, and later they were supplemented by Anglo-Saxon settlers pushing into eastern Scotland from Northumbria.

At no point in this early history was Scotland considered as a political, cultural or even geographical concept. These early societies were all kin based, with tribal chiefs merging into territorial groupings through shifting allegiances to particular sub-kings and high kings. The Picts were divided into two spheres of influence, northern and southern. The Dalriadan Celts in Argyll defined themselves as different from – yet related to – Irish Dalriada. The Brythonic Celts of southern Scotland had three tribal kingdoms. All of these groupings fought with each other, but often made alliances and intermarried. They also looked beyond their borders, connecting through trading and raiding with Britain and the Continent.

One legacy of the Roman period, perhaps little noticed at the time amid a diversity of religious practice, was the arrival of Christianity. As the Roman Empire shrank and withdrew, this new religion sowed the seeds of a different kind of political and cultural order, which was later to become decisive in the emergence of Scotland as a nation. Meantime, however, the southern Celtic kingdoms struggled to sustain a post-Roman society, while the Pictish kingdoms and Dalriada continued much as before.

However, a steady increase in Anglo-Saxon settlement sought to fill the gap left by the Roman withdrawal, causing a new era of conflict and rivalry from the fourth century onwards. Gradually the southern Celts succumbed to the expanding Anglian kingdom of Northumbria, while the Picts and Dalriadans fought, sometimes in alliance, to resist further expansion. This period gave birth to the legends of Arthur, a warrior chief who led mobile cavalry against the Saxons, and upheld a late Romano-Christian culture in opposition to 'the heathen' barbarians.

Subsequently Picts, Dalriadans and Anglians all adopted Christianity and applied its growing European prestige to bolster their own rulers. Key missionaries, including Ninian of

Whithorn, Columba of Iona, and Kentigern of Strathclyde, left their mark on Scotland's national story. But this was not part of their own immediate purpose, which was to Christianize the various kingdoms and confederacies which held regional sway.

The turning point in this story came in about 800, when Norse raids around the coasts of Scotland began in earnest. These heralded two centuries of incursion, invasion and settlement affecting all parts of the Scottish territories, not just the far north as is often believed. In consequence the two great regional powers – the Dalriadans who had come to be generally known as 'the Scots', and the Picts – moved closer together. They now faced a formidable common enemy and the previous shifting alliances took firmer shape in terms of military muscle and of dynastic connections.

Dalriada's concept of kingship was strongly influenced by the Irish tradition of High Kingship. In addition this indigenous Irish model had been influenced and reinforced by the Christian idea that a king, like a Christian emperor, could be ordained and upheld by God. The prestige of these Dalriadan ideas ensured that when a joint Kingship of Picts and Scots emerged, its cultural expressions were Scots and Gaelic. This led eventually to the loss of the Pictish language, leaving us the tantalizing riches of their monumental carvings and symbol stones, without their contextual meaning.

However, this alliance of Picts, Scots and Christianity proved in time effective, and though Norse influence in Scotland became a permanent and enriching legacy, Scottish territory was not swallowed up by one of the Viking empires. On the contrary, the idea of a Scottish nation had been born.

The Kingship of Picts and Scots was well documented in the early medieval annals, but took its full place on the European stage with the marriage in 1066 of Malcolm Canmore, King of Scots, to the Saxon Princess Margaret, who was fleeing from the Norman invasion of England. This alliance inaugurated a new form of Church–state alliance in the European mould, and laid the foundations of a thriving medieval Scottish kingdom.

Like most medieval kingdoms, this was less a unitary state than a collection of territories ruled by an increasingly powerful monarch backed up by a court administration. The monarch reigned through powers of patronage and justice combined with force when necessary. Conflict between regional lords and the monarch were commonplace, and Highland and island areas continued to be ruled in Gaelic style with little recognition of central royal government.

None the less, the Scottish monarchy proved remarkably stable, until the line of Malcolm and Margaret petered out following the death of Alexander III at Kinghorn in 1286. He fell off a cliff trying to reach his young, but as yet childless, wife. The heir was a little Norwegian princess and when she too died en route to Scotland, the first second crisis of Scottish independence began. Norse incursions count as the first.

The story so far concerns remote history, but the 60-year battle for independence that began at Kinghorn still resonates. It is how people remember the history that counts as much as the history, and this story of patriotic struggle runs deep. The Scottish Independence Referendum in 2014 coincides with the 700th anniversary of the Battle of Bannockburn in 1314; the nearest Scotland has come so far to a national anthem is the Bannockburn-inspired 'Flower of Scotland' sung lustily before rugby matches. Robert the Bruce, King of Scots, and William Wallace, Guardian of Scotland, were and are national heroes.

The nub of that historical struggle lies in the relationship between England and Scotland, which is where the heart of the matter still rests. These neighbouring kingdoms had warred intermittently, and sometimes made alliances through royal marriage in the tried and tested medieval manner. But there was an underlying and nagging problem. England had continental ambitions, not least because their royal house also held territory in France. But if an English king was committed to continental wars, it was highly inconvenient if a lesser Scottish monarch could demonstrate Scotland's independence by coming over the land border to threaten England from the rear.

By 1286 many of the Scottish nobility, including the Bruces, were of Norman descent and also had landholdings in England. Some had been on crusade with the young Prince Edward, now Edward I, and it seemed natural to turn to this related monarch to help resolve the succession crisis. What the Scots seem to have missed is that Edward Plantaganet was a formidable military and political operator. Following the successful annexation of Wales, albeit in the teeth of fierce native opposition, he was intent on reviving a long-running claim to overlordship of Scotland. Edward ruled in favour of one of the contestants, John Baliol, because he believed the Baliols would concur in the subordination of Scotland to the English crown.

What Edward for his part underestimated was the strength of Scottish loyalty to 'the community of the realm of Scotland', which underpinned the Scottish version of constitutional monarchy. In addition, Edward had not fully grasped the ungraspability of Scotland's extensive and rugged terrain. In the face of even modest resistance the kingdom became ungovernable. The consequence of these miscalculations on both sides was a long and bloody conflict that continued well beyond Bannockburn and Robert the Bruce's death.

But the long struggle was not just military: it was also political and constitutional. Both sides resorted to Rome, the UN of the day, to present their case. Both dug into legend and tradition to concoct a mythic lineage for their national status and claims. The English side drew on a foundation legend linking England to Rome, and ultimately Troy through descent from Brutus. This, claimed the English theologians and lawyers was, the origin of Britain as a unified kingdom to which Scotland and Wales were subordinate.

The Scots, by contrast, dug into the traditions that had come from Dalriada to the Kingdom of the Scots and Picts. In this legend Scotland trumped the English claims by going back to the Old Testament. Their progenitrix was none other than a daughter of Pharaoh who had aided the escape of the children of Israel. Fleeing Egyptian wrath along with her Greek consort, Scota came to Scotland via Spain and Ireland. The Stone of Destiny on which kings were crowned at Scone came by the same route and demonstrated the ancient legitimacy of the Scottish monarchy.

These mythic claims seem incredible to modern ears, but in a society based on royal legitimacy they carried weight. In fact, neither version at the time delivered a constitutional game changer. Yet Edward I did seize the Stone of Destiny and transport it to Westminster Abbey where it rested under the coronation chair until 1950 when it was removed by a group of young nationalists. Finally in 1996 the Stone was returned to Scotland on condition that it would be made available again to Westminster for a coronation, an agreement that may soon be tested.

According to some historians, Edward did not get the real Stone which had been hidden by the Abbot of Scone. Legends breed legends echoing through the centuries but, power of legend aside, Scottish independence was retained through an extended and costly war of attrition.

When normal business was finally restored, the medieval Scottish monarchy, which had moved through marriage from Bruces to Stewarts, continued amid a fractious nobility, assassinations, marriage alliances and English fall-outs. Despite the instabilities and bloodletting, Scots still regard the Stewart monarchs with affection. This was a period when the expanding Scottish burghs nurtured new forms of town life, there was economic growth, and the royal palaces at Stirling, Holyrood, Falkland and Linlithgow were developed into the significant landmarks that they remain today. Kingship was felt to be an institution that was close to the people.

But the Stewart dynasty led to the Union of the Crowns of Scotland and England in 1603, and the removal of the Court to London in the person of James VI of Scotland and I of Britain and Ireland. His claim to both crowns came through his mother Mary, the deposed Queen of Scots, who had been conveniently executed by the English. In effect Scotland's king turned the monarchy into the Protestant British institution we know today and that remains a cornerstone of constitutional unity. Most proposals for Scottish independence, including those of the SNP, include retention of the monarchy. How did this happen? The causes are both political and religious.

The idea of joining the two monarchies through marriage was nothing new, but it was Henry VIII who set in motion the events that changed this from a generational into a near permanent solution to the conundrum of two kingdoms sharing one island. Henry's sister Margaret was already married to James IV of Scotland in what was hailed as the twining of the thistle and the rose, but that did not prevent the two nations going to war in 1513 with disastrous consequences for Scotland at the Battle of Flodden. It was Henry's need for an heir, combined with his outsized European ambitions, that led to the English Reformation and the introduction of religious difference as a potent force in Britain's dynastic politics.

According to Roman Catholic legitimists, the heir to the English throne after the death of Mary Tudor was Mary Stewart, only child of James V of Scotland. Instead a now avowedly Protestant England placed Anne Boleyn's daughter Elizabeth on the throne. This proved a long-lasting but ultimately temporary expedient, as Elizabeth did not marry and had no offspring. This once again left Mary Stewart Queen of Scots – and for a time of France too – in pole position. To the English administration led by William Cecil, Mary's Catholicism and her ties to France were a grievous threat.

When Mary returned to Scotland in 1561 to take up the reins of government, Scotland was in the throes of its own Protestant Reformation. Though constrained by Elizabeth's devotion to the rights of legitimate monarchs, Cecil set about systematically and ruthlessly undermining Mary's government. In this he was aided by the ever factious Scottish nobility, not least Mary's own illegitimate half-brother James Stewart and, by Mary's marriage to the disastrous Henry Stewart, Lord Darnley. After the birth of Mary's first and only child, James, Darnley was assassinated in still unexplained circumstances. This resulted in Mary's deposition and flight to England, where

Cecil promptly had her imprisoned until he could persuade a reluctant Elizabeth to chop off her head.

Darnley himself had a claim to both thrones through his descent from the same Margaret Tudor who had married James IV. In consequence, Mary's son by Darnley was in an unrivalled position to succeed to the throne in England and Scotland. The only potential obstacle was that James had been baptized by Mary as a Catholic, but the Protestant Regents now in power in Scotland ensured that he was brought up as a Protestant. Though James himself remained ecumenical in matters of religion, he was very keen to escape the clutches of his fractious nobles, and when he grew up the young Scottish king was determined to secure the English crown even at the expense of disowning his mother's rights.

Consequently in 1603 when the aged Elizabeth finally expired, James departed for London, returning only once to Scotland in the course of a long reign. This Union of the Crowns was unpopular in Scotland and in England; it was driven by what was seen as political and religious necessity in face of the hostile European powers. Ironically, what had been held up as the solution to the problem of war and disunity in Britain was to result in the worst civil wars ever to occur in the united kingdoms of England, Scotland and Ireland.

James VI, of Scotland, and I of Great Britain and Ireland, was probably the most intelligent and cultured individual ever to occupy the throne. We owe to him the Authorized Version of the Bible and the mature flourishing of Shakespeare's art. But James's political views were resolutely monarchical, formed in reaction to his own upbringing by adherents of the Presbyterian version of limited kingship. James instructed his children in the divine right of kings to rule directly under God. Charles I, who succeeded his father, imbibed this lesson well, and died for these principles like his grandmother, Mary Queen of Scots.

The titanic struggles between different versions of monarchy and parliamentary rule, backed up by contrasting forms of religious justification, continued through the bloody and discordant seventeenth century in Britain and across Europe. In Scotland resistance to the Stewart monarchs combined religion and politics in the National Covenant of 1638, which bound the nation under God to overthrow tyranny and establish a godly commonwealth by force if necessary.

Concepts formed in the Reformation and Covenanting periods passed into later political thought and remain influential. Amid these is the idea that sovereignty or ultimate legitimacy lies with the people (or at least the religiously covenanted people) rather than in the institutions of monarchy or parliament. This idea can be traced back to the medieval 'Declaration of Arbroath' which was submitted to Rome as part of the Scottish case for independence. The twentieth-century movement for Scottish Home Rule, which led to the Devolution Referendum in 1997, was also consciously rooted in the right of the Scottish people to exercise a sovereign choice, through modern democratic means.

More immediately, the seventeenth-century struggles led to a Union of the English and Scottish Parliaments in addition to that of the crowns. This happened because, as the parliaments gained in power in their respective jurisdictions, there was a risk that they might make different decisions about royal succession and so break the already existing Union of the Crowns. This was a realistic possibility as many in Scotland regarded James VII and II, who had been deposed in 1688 because of his espousal of Catholic and divine right principles, as their legitimate monarch. So began the Jacobite movement. The Protestant and mercantile elites in both kingdoms had to close down this possible divergence, and so drove through the 'incorporating union' of 1706–7. Their case was based on the benefits to trade alongside political and religious necessity.

This parliamentary union was deeply unpopular in both countries. For many, though, it came just in time to secure the Protestant succession of the German-speaking Elector of Hanover as George I in 1712. Queen Anne had added to Stewart (now Stuart) woes by dying without surviving offspring so, bypassing the senior male line of the Catholic James VII, hereditary right was linked back to the female descendants of James VI and I.

In this way, a political solution fashioned for the advantage of the Stuart dynasty finally led to its displacement. None the less, the 1707 Treaty of Union did preserve royal authority into the modern political era, though the monarch's sovereignty was to a significant degree vested in the new Westminster Parliament. England could console itself that, though Scottish representation was now mandatory, in most essentials the English Parliament continued. To this day the monarch opens Parliament and announces the measures that 'our government' will enact in the coming session. Technically a Prime Minister of the UK can declare war or form a new government on the basis of a royal rather than a democratic mandate.

In some ways the Treaty of Union between England and Scotland is the nearest Britain comes to having a written constitution. It still has a unique importance in the constitutional arrangements of the UK. Unravelling it would have as many implications for the other parts of the existing UK as it does for Scotland.

The 1707 Union ushered in modern Britain, and in retrospect the beginnings of both industry and empire can be traced back to this period. In the immediate aftermath, though, the trading benefits that had been promised were slow to materialize. There were anti-Scottish riots in London and anti-London riots in Edinburgh. The threat of nationalist revolt to restore the Stuarts loomed large. However, although the Jacobites almost succeeded in 1715, and came close to London in the rising of 1745, their cause was progressively overtaken by economic and social change.

From the mid-eighteenth century Scotland experienced accelerating economic growth. The conjunction of raw materials such as coal and iron ore, combined with access to capital and a disposition to education and hard work, made Scotland a powerhouse of industrialization. At the same time the expansion of British interests overseas provided new markets and access to resources of all kinds. To the shame of both Scotland and England these resources included slave labour. The Industrial Revolution was underway.

The social impact on Scotland was disproportionate. Traditional hierarchies and social obligations disappeared with frightening rapidity, not least in the Highlands where Gaelic culture was suppressed and hereditary chiefs turned into landlords. Populations were uprooted, migrating to the expanding cities at home or expanding colonies abroad. Gradually these changes did bring improved material well-being and life expectancy, but at the expense of a new urban labouring class which lived in squalid conditions without the support of the older communal traditions. The consequences of this upheaval are still part of Scotland's life today, because the same social groups have repeatedly been at the hard end of economic change while largely disenfranchised from its benefits.

Politically Jacobitism and nationalism were sidelined by the struggle to widen the voting franchise in response to changing social dynamics. The 1707 Union froze Scottish parliamentary representation in aspic, so that even in 1832 Scottish MPs were still being elected by tiny handfuls of electors often swayed by bribery. As the poetry of Robert Burns shows, the French Revolution inspired movements for radical reform which in turn provoked violent repression. But eventually the franchise was widened and parliamentary politics took increasing account of public opinion. John Knox's dream of a literate public was also gradually being realized as universal education crept nearer. Democratization and education moved forward together, though in the event weekly newspapers were as much in favour as the Bible.

Urban life also began to generate its own forms of communal solidarity. Religion expanded hugely in the shape of new and existing denominations, along with related anti-temperance, missionary and co-operative movements. Friendly societies – and then trade unions – took shape, and as the franchise was extended political parties looked beyond their insider networks for popular support. The suffragettes pushed for the enfranchisement of women, though this was seen at the time as an inclusion too far.

Despite cyclical ups and downs, Britain grew wealthier due to its expanding empire and technological innovation. Scotland was a junior but very active partner in the imperial project providing industrial muscle and investing in the colonies with people, capital and military manpower. Already in the 1820s Sir Walter Scott had declared Scottish history over, subsumed into Britain's imperial project. Why then did Scotland survive as more than a historical footnote or, in Scott's version, as a source of Romantic loyalties?

In the eighteenth and nineteenth centuries, *The Scots Magazine* carried information about deaths, births and weddings from around the world. Publication was seen as a vital way of disseminating family information and of keeping up connections despite being separated by large distances. Kith and kin still mattered profoundly, and the main purpose of empire for most Scots was to advance family members through colonial jobs and opportunities. A Scots diaspora operated within the imperial system, and has in some ways survived it as 'heritage Scots' still identify with their origins, sporting vivid tartan markers of Scottish identity.

By the middle of the nineteenth century two versions of Scottishness were gaining traction simultaneously. British tartanry was enthusiastically harnessed to the imperial cause, reaching a royal apogee as Queen Victoria identified the monarchy with the Scottish Highlands at Balmoral. But at the same time a distinctly anti-imperial movement for Scottish Home Rule was underway. Paradoxically both sides shared an interest in history and heritage. Scottishness was cultivated in ways that would have baffled previous generations. In 1867 the Wallace Monument was ceremoniously opened after a huge civic effort, uniting miners, aristocrats and European 'liberators' such as Garibaldi. In 1885 the Westminster government decided to create a department for Scotland with a Scottish Secretary sitting in the Cabinet.

This divide between versions of Scottishness opened up more sharply in the 1880s as Home Rule for Ireland defined the battle lines of British politics, Liberal and Conservative. Next up was the Boer War in South Africa, during which many Scottish Liberals opposed British imperial policy. Not until the onset of

World War One in 1914 did Scotland swing again wholeheart-edly behind the patriotic line, though even then Glasgow was a hotbed of radical protest and dissent.

In retrospect 'the war to end wars' proved a watershed for Scottish society. The huge losses sustained, disproportion-ately in Scotland where military service was deeply engrained, brought imperial optimism to a shuddering halt. The 'for God and country' ideology that had dominated the nineteenth century stagnated in the face of, first, horrific loss of life and subsequently destructive economic depression. The impact of prolonged depression on rural areas, which had already given so many lives on the western front, was particularly devastat-ing. But urban areas offered no compensating opportunities, and new waves of emigration began.

In the aftermath of World War One, the US President Woodrow Wilson promoted the principle of national 'self-determination', which was enshrined in the new international mechanism of the League of Nations. At the same time, the punitive reparations imposed on Germany, at the insistence of France and Britain, sowed the seeds of Nazism and another global conflict.

In the 1920s Scottish Nationalism emerged as a distinct though marginal political movement. The poetry of Hugh Mac-Diarmid and others sparked a Scottish cultural renaissance with strong political overtones. Meanwhile, work was progressing on an ambitious National War Memorial in Edinburgh Castle, followed by a major new administrative centre for the Scot-tish Office in Edinburgh – the monumental St Andrew's House on Calton Hill. In retrospect this seems a period of contradic-tion and unease. Victory appeared to have secured the British Empire, but in reality global leadership was already passing to the USA.

In 1939 Britain reluctantly went to war once more to combat Hitler. It was a necessary cause but not one for enthusiastic, imperial patriotism. While Churchill manoeuvred to maintain postwar influence, Scottish attention was focused on recon-structing a more just social order and achieving new economic investment. The work of Tom Johnston, Scotland's wartime Secretary of State, fostered a new sense of Scotland's potential.

Nationalists and advocates of Home Rule united in the post-war Scottish Covenant of 1949–50. Signed by two million Scots and delivered to Downing Street, this restated the historic claim to self-government, at a time when Canada, Australia, South Africa and New Zealand were all moving towards self-governing Dominion status. But neither of the two major forces in British politics, Conservative and Labour, had any interest in ceding power to Scotland, while Scottish representation, which was balanced between the parties, had no hope of swaying parliamentary majorities in London.

The austere postwar years ground on until a degree of economic growth was restored in the 1950s. The consumer rather than the citizen became the focus of political attention. In reality Britain's economy continued to stagnate compared to the advances in Europe, North America and Japan. The Suez debacle of 1959, when Britain invaded Egypt to crush a nationalist revolt but had to withdraw on US orders, cruelly exposed how threadbare the mantle of British world power had become. The Empire continued to melt away without the UK discovering a new role.

Political attention in the 1960s and 1970s was focused on Britain's continuing economic woes, and its in-out relationship with Europe, until the discovery of oil in the North Sea reignited Scottish political debate. Under the slogan 'It's Scotland's oil', the SNP started to win even in Labour heartlands. Despite deep internal divisions, the Labour government of the day pushed ahead with legislation for a 'Scottish Assembly' which would be given non tax-raising powers over domestic Scottish affairs.

At this critical juncture, English political representation at Westminster, working on a cross-party basis, exercised a veto. Backbench Labour dissenters combined with the Conservatives to rule that the Assembly could only proceed if at least 40 per cent of those eligible to vote, as opposed to those actually voting, approved. Few recent governments would have been elected on this basis.

In the event, after a dour and divisive campaign, a decisive majority voted in favour but still fell short of 40 per cent of those on the electoral register. In the course of the campaign former Prime Minister Sir Alec Douglas-Home, whose ancestors were instrumental in the 1707 Union, urged Scots to reject these 'flawed' proposals and pledged that the Conservative Party would do better. Later in 1979 Labour lost a confidence motion in the Commons, and in the ensuing election Mrs Thatcher came to power, beginning 17 years of Conservative rule, during which no further proposals for Scottish devolution were forthcoming.

The failed Referendum of 1979 left a sour taste in Scottish public life. One casualty of the backlash was the SNP which endured electoral losses and internal splits. But the devolution aftermath was rapidly overtaken by more immediate alarms, as the Thatcher government embarked on major structural changes in the British economy along with legislation to undermine trade union power.

In initiating these radical reforms, there was no consideration in Westminster of any Scottish dimension. Along with other heavily industrialized areas dependent on working-class manual employment, Scotland suffered disproportionately as traditional industries went into steep decline. Interest rates and unemployment soared, blighting the lives of whole communities. The legacy of disempowerment and anger was all too visible in the national miners' strike of 1984. But the damage to Scotland's social fabric was pervasive and long lasting as the housing schemes created by earlier social engineering became subject to unemployment, drug addiction, and the breakdown of family support structures.

The 1980s cruelly exposed Scotland's over-reliance on heavy industries unfitted to meet new global competition. In addition, many of the social problems were a cumulative inheritance from earlier industrialization. Some people benefited from the Thatcher emphasis on private ownership and wealth, but the realignments were too sudden and lacking in compensating initiatives or investment. Oil revenues and other public assets were diverted to fund election-winning tax cuts.

The lesson for most Scots, finally driven home by the early introduction in Scotland of the Community Charge or Poll Tax, was that some form of self-government was now a necessity. As 17 years of Conservative government rolled on, the party disappeared from Scotland's electoral map. Yet Scotland's democratic dissent failed to dent Mrs Thatcher's landslide victories in England. John Major's administration did introduce some further measures of administrative devolution to the Scottish Office, and in 1996 the Scottish Secretary Michael Forsyth returned the Stone of Destiny to Scotland on loan. But by then it was too late. Mrs Thatcher's claim that, after the Falklands War, Great Britain was great again had fallen on deaf ears north of the border.

The next push for Home Rule was carefully prepared with politicians working across political divides, and involving trade unions, churches and other representatives of 'civic society'. A Constitutional Convention was convened and although the SNP did not participate, they did eventually join the campaign in support of its outcomes. The Convention's 'Claim of Right' restated the traditional Scottish understanding of 'the sovereignty of the people'. Most of the participants believed they were reclaiming some part of what had been given up in 1707.

Labour politicians such as John McIntosh, John Smith – who was for a short time Labour's leader before his early death – and Donald Dewar were prominent devolution advocates. When Labour swept to power at Westminster in 1997 under Smith's successor Tony Blair, the devolution's long awaited moment had finally arrived. In 1997, untrammelled by any percentage rule, the electorate voted overwhelmingly for a Scottish Parliament with some tax-raising powers.

However, what was conceded to Scotland in 1997 did not reverse the 1707 Treaty of Union between England and Scotland, or theoretically lessen the power of the Westminster Parliament. The sovereign British state, embodied in the monarch and through

her vested in Parliament, remitted the exercise of some of its powers to Edinburgh. The same Parliament could legislate to recover
those devolved powers if desired. This perspective is reflected in
the title of 'Scottish Executive', which was accorded the new Parliament's executive arm. This was not a fully fledged government:
Scotland was no longer entirely stateless, but it was not a state.

Despite this, at the opening session in 1999, veteran nationalist Winnie Ewing spoke deliberately of the Scottish Parliament being reconvened. And the rapidity with which the new
Parliament was accepted as the leading institution in Scottish
life is remarkable given the 300-year gap. When a minority
nationalist administration gained power in 2007, one of its first
acts was to rename itself, to general public acceptance, as the
Scottish Government.

When in 2011, against the odds, the SNP won an outright
majority, the scene was set for a Referendum on Scottish independence. Inevitably this process is beset by arguments about
legality, content and potential outcomes. The state Scotland is
in now was conditioned by centuries of unique development.
All the circumstances and issues culminate in the question
'What does independence mean, and what kind of state might
Scotland become?'

# 2

# A Scottish Question

Identity is the sense of our selves, past, present and future. It is personal, familial and collective. The question, however, is why Scotland's sense of identity has persisted in some form through so many social and political changes.

The pioneering sociologist and ecologist Patrick Geddes, a passionate Scot and internationalist, argued that identity is a cultural result of the way in which people, places and ways of living interact with one another. Human life and the natural environment together shape social structures and the cultural character of communities. The cut and thrust of political fortunes, Geddes implies, is more subject to long-term influences than might be apparent at first sight. 'By leaves we live' was a Geddes maxim, along with 'think global, act local'.

This approach is apt for a Scotland where climate, landscape, flora and fauna are so distinctive, and influential on all aspects of human life. Geography dictated the patterns of early settlement in Scotland, while even in a more mobile era, life in Scotland has to accommodate weather and location regardless of people's origins. In addition, the relationship between natural resources and human society is at the centre of current debate about political and economic options. Oil, water, gas, fish, deer, bees, trees and genes, to name but a few, are hot topics of debate with big consequences for Scotland's economics, politics and culture. In the present era of global climate change, these questions are also ethical.

Spirituality too has a part to play in self-understanding, and in our sense of how the wider contexts of life impinge on human consciousness. This dimension is often implicit and unexpressed, though it may also be expressed through deliberate reflection or meditation. Spirituality understood in this way is different from the social practice of religion, though religions can shape or in turn be influenced by forms of spirituality.

Considering all these aspects, how is Scotland's sense of itself expressed? And how can this sustained Scottish identity be characterized?

Scotland's mountainous terrain, criss-crossed by often fertile river valleys, studded with lochs, and surrounded by islanded seas, occupies the imagination of most inhabitants and many exiles. It is a striking landscape which contains within its overall drama much local diversity. Travelling in Scotland is an experience of contrast and sometimes challenge.

In the twentieth century it was fashionable to criticize the attachment of Scots to the natural world as 'sentimental'. After all, the majority of modern Scots are urban dwellers, so was it not nostalgic and anachronistic to have strong emotional connection with 'the land'? This critique of course ignores the reality that every Scottish city from Aberdeen to Glasgow is sited because of primary natural features and resources. Most urban Scots retain a strong realistic sense of their natural hinterland, while many leisure activities are focused on reconnecting with the countryside through walking, fishing, gardening, climbing, bird-watching or sailing.

However, metropolitan superiority about nature-loving Scottishness has been overtaken by the global environmental crisis. Far from being quaint, Scottish identification with the natural environment now seems vital, forward-looking, and even trendsetting. To love nature is to love life. The twenty-first-century perspective moves away from humanity as the master of nature to a model of partnership, stewardship and collaboration. But it is also an inner sense of connection that sets our self-consciousness on the edge of something bigger and deeper. All life is fragile but consciousness is especially vulnerable and precious, existing on spiritual borderlands between mind and matter.

Scottish poets return to this theme again and again. Norman MacCaig, the poet of Assynt in Sutherland, is also a celebrated part of Edinburgh's literary life. While walking in the capital 'sprawling like seven cats/on its seven hills beside the Firth of Forth', he is 'amongst the mountains and lochs of that corner/ that looks across the Minch to the Hebrides'. Both are precious gifts central to his poetic inspiration.

Beyond pure moments of contemplation and insight such as poets sometimes enjoy, human awareness of nature is connected with cultural and personal memories. The landscape is a repository of our histories, where natural heritage and human stories combine.

History and heritage play a large part in Scottish identity. Again this has been criticized as backward-looking and distorting. Scots have been accused of peddling a version of themselves through the heritage industry that is skewed and even dishonest. Yet how people represent and interpret history is the bedrock of heritage, and cultural representation is part of historical understanding. There is no pure history without interpretation.

Some of the complications are evident in the history of tartan. Tartanry has been described as a nineteenth-century invention, providing a substitute form of identity in a period when Scotland's political and social distinctiveness had waned. But tartan has a long history: even Roman relief sculpture shows Celtic warriors wearing a garment of checked fabric that is clearly an ancestor of the kilt. The nineteenth century reinterpreted and re-presented tartan, as did the twentieth, and at the start of the twenty-first century there are many bold re-appropriations of tartan in fashion and fabrics. Is that not healthy and creative cultural evolution? Should each generation not reinterpret its heritage in new ways?

One litmus test is whether increased historical knowledge diminishes Scotland's attachment to heritage. The opposite applies. As archaeologists and historians have expanded and diversified their understanding of Scotland's past, from Palaeolithic hunter gatherers to African migrants, the thirst for more interpretation and more participative heritage experiences has grown. The Scottish historical narrative has become more appealing as it has grown richer in detail and complexity.

There seems to be a correlation between the diverse riches of Scotland's natural ecology and the variety and depth of the country's historical inheritance. Together they provide local, regional, national and international perspectives on who the Scots now are, or think they are. Like biological genes, the past is always with us, influencing and shaping the present. Scottish culture tends to embrace that dimension of identity with enthusiasm. Visitors perceive this aspect of Scotland as genuine, and genuinely important for Scots. This in turn makes it more appealing to outsiders and to those diaspora Scots who may come with fixed idea of Scottishness, yet find a cultural bridge to more complex realities.

Given the diversity of sources, and of interpretations, Scotland's sense of heritage is not monolithic. On the contrary, history is a locus for debate and disagreement. What is the significance of Scotland's constitutional history for the independence question? What is the present status of the Treaty of Union? Were the eighteenth-century Jacobite Risings backward-looking or a vigorous expression of nationalism? Does the life of Keir Hardie, founder of both the Labour Party and a Scottish national movement, show that nationalism and socialism can be happy bedfellows? And so on. Heritage is contested ground, and healthily so. This argumentative strain shows that the past is not a dead cultural hand, but an integral part of dynamic creative thinking.

Religion is another contested aspect of identity. The previous chapter has already touched on the part played by institutional religion in Scotland's national evolution, and this topic will be explored more fully in relation to formal statehood in the next. But organized religion has also influenced the social and psychological tenor of Scottish life.

It is inaccurate to say that Scotland has always been a particularly religious society. In early centuries religious practices were an important aspect of communal life, as in most cultures.

But even in the medieval period, when the Christian Church was the main institution in Scotland, it is hard to gauge how deeply or widely belief was held across the population. Adherence for many may have been quite nominal, attending mass once a year at Easter and paying the Church's dues. After the Protestant Reformation in 1560, a long process of education and evangelization began, but John Knox's 'godly commonwealth' was always an ideal and, even in its seventeenth-century heyday, Calvinist piety was a minority pursuit.

Ironically, it seems to have been the break-up of traditional communities and the rapid growth of cities that turned Christianity into a true mass movement in Scotland. This involved a variety of Protestant denominations and the renaissance of Roman Catholicism. Many people were economic migrants, and in the harsh urban conditions, organized religion offered alternative forms of identity and solidarity. Religious activism addressed social as well as spiritual needs, as many people must have felt alienated and despairing in the face of disease, grinding poverty and environmental degradation. Alcholism became a common means of escape.

Did mass religion generate life-affirming change or repress individual creativity in favour of passive social conformity? There are examples of both, but certainly by the mid-twentieth century the emphasis was on conformity, flagged up by the Churches' hopeless attempt to roll back the 'permissive society'. Perhaps in the nineteenth century religion was more of a force for change, even though it rarely challenged the economic and political order directly. However, whether passive or active, organized religion had become a prominent marker of social and personal identity.

It is also possible that in the absence of a strong Scottish political construct, the major Christian traditions provided a partial substitute. This may throw some light on the tenacity of religious sectarianism in Scottish society even after the waning of active Christian belief. For Irish and Italian immigrants the Catholic Church was a primary allegiance, while most of the Protestant denominations promoted Britishness as a combined political and religious loyalty. By comparison, a shared sense of Scottishness was relatively weak from the late eighteenth until the mid-twentieth centuries. Religious allegiance was a more powerful marker.

Cumulatively these factors could have led to a lack of psychological confidence in Scottish society and an inclination towards defensive, conservative pessimism. Low aspiration was concealed by blaming the environment. The idea that to 'get on' people had to break out and leave was a pervasive attitude, when life for the majority was a constant physical struggle. At the same time, there is plenty of evidence for Scottish innovation, enterprise and radicalism in the modern period, so a blanket diagnosis of failing confidence may risk reinforcing the pessimism it aims to overturn. It is more likely that very specific economic and social problems resulted in poor health, physically and psychologically, for a significant number of people.

If the social focus of religious organizations in the past dampened individuality, contemporary spirituality strongly emphasizes the individual. Alternative therapies linked with nature, art or music are also an alternative to religion, emphasizing personal choice and fulfilment.

The same trend can be seen in wider questions about identity. The consuming interest in genealogy, now backed up by genetic mapping, links quests for personal fulfilment, or at least knowledge, with heritage. This is another example of how the past can be harnessed to many different expressions of identity. Family connection, however remote, carries strong emotional appeal in the present individualistic ethos.

What remains unclear is the extent to which an independent Scotland would continue older collective loyalties in new ways. Or does the potential appeal of greater political independence lie in a hope for participation in a more personally fulfilling social ethos? The political trick may lie in tapping into a variety of aspirations without ruling out any option. As in many other regards, the independence argument, like the devolution debate, is a laboratory of change rather than the assertion of something fixed and resolved.

All the influences on Scottish identity that have been outlined will play some part in the next stage of Scotland's political development, whatever that may be.

# 3

# Statehood and Religion

Setting aside for the moment questions of identity and spirituality in the broader sense, is there a specifically religious dimension to the question of statehood? The same question might apply to all the options for greater political autonomy in Scotland. And the answer in all cases is yes, though many may be impatient and even irritated that it should be so. But the problem with neglected questions is that they may come back to bite you.

Present-day Scotland is characterized by religious diversity. While agnosticism may command the support of a silent majority, there is an articulate camp of atheistic belief, and a much larger but segmented community of faiths.

There are first of all four Christian denominations in Scotland that consider themselves in some way as direct heirs of historic Christianity. The Orthodox Communion, though variegated as Greek, Russian or Romanian, is a small minority in Scotland, yet one claiming direct descent from the undivided primitive Church of the Mediterranean. This is not irrelevant to Christian origins in Scotland, since the apostolic or first missionary period of Scottish Christianity has strong links with the eastern Mediterranean world. The Celtic saints were familiar and connected with the spiritual fathers and mothers of the monastic traditions in Syria, Egypt and Palestine. The Coptic Church, which is also present in Scotland, belongs to the same cultural world. Andrew, Scotland's national saint, is shared with Russia and Greece.

However, the main medieval development of the Scottish Church with its diocesan and parish structure, which survives in an attenuated form to this day, is a fruit of the Western medieval Church headquartered in Rome. The continuity between the Church of luminaries such as St Margaret of Scotland, Adam of Dryburgh or Bishop Elphinstone and twenty-first-century Roman Catholicism is fragile but real. Though some communities in the Western Isles and the Highlands, and some families, sustained their faith traditions through the long period of persecution, the majority of Scottish Catholics are descended from Irish, Italian or Polish immigrants. The nineteenth-century renaissance of Scottish Catholicism, and its steady consolidation throughout the twentieth century, have placed the Catholic tradition in the front rank of organized Christianity in Scotland, equal in terms of active participation with mainstream Protestantism.

Two mainstream Protestant Churches claim direct descent both from apostolic Christianity and the Reformation of 1560. They are the Presbyterian Church of Scotland and the Scottish Episcopal Church. It was 1690 before the long-running Protestant struggle between Episcopacy and Presbyterianism was settled in favour of a Presbyterian Kirk 'by law established', something that pleased neither the many Episcopal loyalists nor radical Covenanters who wanted a holy, covenanted nation rather than a legally constituted national Church of whatever variety. The question of national status and role will be discussed shortly, but both the small Episcopal Church and the much larger, albeit rapidly declining, Church of Scotland wear some part of the Reformation mantle.

But this is far from the end of the story. The Church of Scotland, in its Presbyterian identity, has a long history of splits and secessions. Many of these relate to the thorny issue of Church–state relations, and others to questions of theological change and development. Today, the United Reformed Church in Scotland, the Free Church of Scotland and the Free Presbyterian Church are offshoots by dispute from the Protestant mainstream and claim some part of its inheritance. Also in radical dissent, but without a claim to any historic succession other than the New

Testament, are Quakers, Baptists, Congregationalists, Methodism in Scotland, Unitarians, Brethren Assemblies and independent evangelical or Pentecostal churches, including Chinese, African and Korean faith communities. In a different category are Mormons and Jehovah's Witnesses, whose interpretation of the Bible derives from modern prophetic movements originating in the United States.

A further dimension of Christian diversity relates to religious orders, ranging from Benedictines to the Society of Jesus, and to centres of retreat and contemplation. While many such orders are Roman Catholic, some are Episcopalian – and even the Church of Scotland gave birth to the now ecumenical Iona Community. More recently Buddhism has added to Scotland's monastic traditions. Staying within Christianity there are also a wide range of para-church movements including everything from Scripture Union to the Orange Order.

The twentieth century brought a significant representation of world religions other than Christianity to Scotland, mainly through migration but with some proselytising. Judaism, Islam, Hinduism, and the Sikh and Bahai faiths are all active in Scotland, though most of these traditions contain, like Christianity, significant internal diversity. Paganism has also been revived as a contemporary religious faith.

This account is not exhaustive but it demonstrates that if Scotland is a secular society, it still embraces a great deal of organized religious activity. This has been recognized by the Scottish Government whose policies welcome religion as a constructive part of civil society. Government and Parliament consult with religious bodies and receive their representations on relevant issues. The Scottish Parliament also reflects Scotland's diversity of faiths in its daily reflections. At the same time, on issues such as same sex unions and euthanasia, the political institutions and some representatives of institutional religion have clashed in fierce disputes.

So if Scotland no longer has a national religion, why does it still have a national Church, albeit one that is not technically called national?

Historically the medieval Christian Church helped create Scotland. It provided a rationale for national kingship, and a social and cultural means of cohering 'the community of the realm', which is how medieval constitutionalists described the kingdom of Scots. This was a predominantly harmonious marriage of Church and state, but in late medieval times strains began to show.

The Church had accumulated huge tracts of land and a lot of disposable wealth. In addition to the dioceses, and parishes, there were well-endowed collegiate churches, monastic foundations and friaries. Meanwhile the relatively weak Scottish monarchy struggled to establish administrative and judicial control over the nobility. For this task money was essential, and successive kings looked to the Church to underwrite their ambitions.

By the time of James V, Protestant reform was a serious and successful European movement, for which James may have harboured some sympathy, but money was his prime focus. By fair means or foul he already had much of the Church's wealth under his control, through the notorious practice of appointing his relatives to lucrative ecclesiastical offices. His illegitimate son, for example, another James Stewart and elder brother to Mary Queen of Scots, was the Prior of St Andrews Cathedral, one of the most richly endowed churches in Scotland.

It was only when the monarchy stalled, after James's premature death, leaving an infant Mary as Queen, that the reformers gained serious traction. As France and England competed for control of the royal baby, radical Protestant ideas took root in the universities and in the burghs. Also many aristocratic families watched events keenly to see if they could use religious politics to grab more land. As the situation see-sawed between French Catholic and English Protestant influences, a decline in Guise influence in France, followed by the death of the Queen Regent, gave the Protestant party the edge.

In 1560, in the absence of either the monarch, who was still in France, or a royally appointed Regent, the 'Thrie Estaitis' of Parliament were persuaded to abolish the authority of the

Pope, outlaw the mass, close the monasteries (many of which had already been looted), and adopt a Confession of Faith devised by six Protestant clerics, one of whom was John Knox. Although these measures lacked royal approval, Mary agreed on her return to Scotland in 1561 not to alter the religious status quo. At the same time she carefully avoided any legal endorsement of the Protestant settlement, leading to the suspicion that she was working to restore the Roman Catholic order, and even to recover some of the lands that the nobility had taken over from the Church. This sowed the seeds of civil war, assassination and, ultimately, Mary's overthrow.

In due course the Protestant Kirk was consolidated and legally established beyond doubt. However, the reformers believed that their new Church was 'established of God', and that they had instructed the terms of their settlement to Parliament on the basis of 'God's Word'. Many in Parliament, particularly the nobility, believed that they had authorized the changes and that the authority replacing the Pope was them, not the preachers. Moreover, Parliament specifically refused to adopt the reformers' radical social and educational blueprint, 'The First Book of Discipline', because it required investing the old Church's wealth for the benefit of the population as a whole. This initial ambiguity set the scene for centuries of conflict.

For a time the competing factions were able to unite to resist Mary and the perceived threat of Roman Catholicism. But as soon as her son James VI assumed personal rule, he worked to re-establish bishops by royal appointment as a means of controlling the Protestants. In opposition to this, reformers – led by Andrew Melville – developed a full-blooded Presbyterian system which excluded bishops and royal power over the Church. The scene was now set for the battles between the Stuart monarchs, soon based in London, and the Covenanters who claimed to uphold the pure 'Kingdom of Christ'. Both sides to this argument, however, believed in the need for one national Church to which everyone owed allegiance – one law, one faith, one Church.

Apart from 1651–60, when Oliver Cromwell absorbed Scotland wholly into Britain, the objective of one authorized

Scottish Church prevailed through the century. Sometimes it was Episcopalian in structure, sometimes Presbyterian, and sometimes both, like two cats in a sack. When William and Mary came to the throne in 1688, they wished to achieve a moderate and inclusive Church settlement in Scotland. Then William was distracted by European wars, and hardline Presbyterians pushed through an exclusive settlement. So a harsh century of conflict ended not with reconciliation, but with another wave of deposed ministers, and congregations ejected from their churches.

All of this was about to play a very significant role in deciding Scotland's constitutional future. The 1690 Williamite settlement moved in the direction of constitutional monarchy and restored powers to the Scottish Parliament. Among these was the right to decide on the succession. Since first William and Mary – and then Mary's sister Queen Anne – lacked heirs, this became critical. A majority in Parliament wanted to use its power not only to secure the succession, but to protect its powers and Scotland's Presbyterian Church order.

In 1703 the Scottish Parliament passed an Act of Security setting out its rights on these matters. This was seen as a hostile measure by the English Parliament and preparations were set in train for war. The situation was aggravated because many in Scotland wanted to restore the legitimate Stewart line, which raised for England the old spectre of a Catholic monarch in Scotland coming to the aid of France, with whom England was once more at war. With some reluctance the governments of England and Scotland swung round to the view that the only way to secure the Protestant succession was to unite the parliaments as well as the crowns.

In this fraught political situation, religion became decisive. The Church began by strongly supporting Scottish autonomy, which guaranteed its own privileged position. But in due course the Church was won over to the idea of Britain by a separate Act, which guaranteed the Protestant religion and Presbyterian Church government. In due course the Act was also engrossed into the Treaty of Union. By this peculiar route, a church system that vehemently insisted on its independence from any form of state control was written into secular law as effectively the national Church. The institution that had been a backbone of Scottish identity since Scotland began was now underwritten through incorporation into the newly united British state.

Many grassroots Presbyterians never caught up with these power plays, and continued to be part of the overwhelming and vociferous popular opposition to union. Moreover, for the radical Covenanters and their heirs, the process was yet one more example of sinful dealings with the secular Satan.

In fact these dissenters were not so far off the mark. Union was implemented in 1707, and in 1712 the Westminster Parliament legislated on Scottish church affairs in direct contradiction to the Treaty and its 'security'. The new law concerned who should appoint parish ministers. Presbyterianism considered it a primary and sacred right of the congregation, as 'the people of God', to choose and elect their minister, who was then introduced to the 'office' by Presbytery. But the historic right of 'Heritors', the landowners who were physically responsible for the churches, to appoint ministers was restored by the 1712 Act. Such patronage was detested by the Presbyterians, and even the Scottish peers in the House of Lords recognized it as a clear breach of the Treaty. But for English aristocrats the idea of 'the populace' choosing the clergy was abhorrent. Parliament was sovereign and Parliament was also largely English, even when it came to the Treaty of Union.

The 1712 Act became a running sore in Scottish ecclesiastical and social life. Numerous secessions resulted from opposition to secular interference or controls. Theological divisions multiplied and communities fragmented, not because the Scots were fatally disputatious, but because government in London did not understand the situation on the ground. As new waves of religious energy swept Britain in the late eighteenth and early nineteenth centuries, the Church of Scotland found itself unable to adapt and respond within the law. Finally in 1843 the Church broke in two over the patronage issue, and a new storm of local secessions and church building was unleashed.

The evidence of all this remains in many Scottish towns and cities where Free Church, Established Church and Secession church buildings jostle with each other, many of them no longer in religious use.

Of course innovative energies were also at play through these conflicts. They fuelled church growth at home and missionary movements abroad. Yet these Presbyterian divisions were overtaken in turn by the expansion of organized religion in more diverse forms. As both Episcopalianism and Roman Catholicism grew in Scotland, along with independent church movements such as Congregationalism, the Presbyterian leaders became concerned about how they were going to retain pole position. In addition, church division was weakening the influence of the churches over vital areas of national life such as education. The government was taking over things that the Church had traditionally overseen, because there were too many discordant religious voices.

By the late nineteenth century the Protestant Churches had begun a long process of reunification. Their aim was to reform and strengthen the national Church as a truly Presbyterian entity, albeit one underpinned by state recognition. Secession and Free Churches came together first, and then the resultant United Free Church of Scotland and the Church of Scotland united in 1929, so restoring numerical superiority over all other religious institutions. At each stage of the process minorities stood out on grounds of theological principle, leaving a cluster of Free, Free Presbyterian and United Free Churches, which agreed neither with the new majority institution, nor with one another.

The way to the grand reunion was paved by the passing at the Westminster Parliament of the Church of Scotland Act (1921), which remains in force. How many legislators understood what it was all about must be a moot point, but the government of the day steered it through on the grounds of Scottish consensus. The 1921 Act affirms the right and responsibility of the Church of Scotland to provide the 'ordinances of religion' in every part of Scotland through the historic system of parishes.

Presbyterian church government is guaranteed, though the theology surrounding the Act, expressed in what are termed the 'Declaratory Articles', is ecumenical, affirming the place of the Church of Scotland in a universal Christian Church.

The immediate consequence of the Act was the 1929 Union or reunion, but there were other practical implications. The new Church's General Assembly became the nearest Scotland had to a representative national assembly, a kind of substitute parliament on some matters at least. It is regrettable that this Assembly used its new influence to mount an anti-Catholic and racist campaign for the repatriation of Irish immigrants in the 1930s. At later points the Assembly played a dignified and even, on issues such as nuclear disarmament, a prophetic role in national life.

On a more practical point the control of heritors over church property was ended, at United Free Church insistence, gradually cutting off many church buildings from traditional sources of support. There were too many churches and too many ministers in the united body, leading to a perpetual process of readjustment, which became locally painful and divisive when decline aggravated the inherited problem of over-supply. Scotland had begun to look like a seriously over-churched society.

A further problem for the twentieth-century Church of Scotland was the wide range of theological views the reunion encompassed. Both Conservatives inclining to literal interpretations and liberal revisionists were all committed to the idea that the Bible, as 'the Word of God', was their supreme rule of life and faith. But in practice the conclusions drawn were contrasting and sometimes conflicting. For a time these differences were masked by the success and sheer size of the Church, which could accommodate diversity within some broad formulaic definitions. But unease set in along with numerical decline. By the late twentieth century attenders were often bypassing their local parish church in favour of one suited to their own theological preferences.

On several occasions the Church of Scotland tried to find a modern Confession of Faith to replace the High Calvinism of its seventeenth-century Westminster Confession, but drew back in face of potential conflict. In consequence the official language of belief progressively parted company from any general understanding in Church or society. Even among ministers versed in historical theology, the Confession chimed with neither liberal nor contemporary evangelical perspectives.

The Church of Scotland's relationship with the British monarchy was a continuing paradox. George V duly gave royal assent to the Church of Scotland Act of 1921, in line with his constitutional duty. By established custom, he already appointed a royal representative to the General Assembly. This 'Lord High Commissioner' still looks down from a grand gallery and is 'invited' to make an address on behalf of the monarch, which is loyally 'received' by the Assembly, though with the implication that the royal message might equally be rejected. The High Commissioner's job has been done by members of the royal family, and on occasions by the monarch. The British Head of State has official status in England as 'Defender of the Faith', but he or she has no official position in the Church of Scotland, which claims it's 'only King and Head, Jesus Christ'.

This official line, however, conceals a strong linkage between Scottish Protestantism, Unionism and the British monarchy. The Church of Scotland's twentieth-century membership had a substantial overlap with the majority vote for the Scottish Unionist (later Conservative and Unionist) Party which dominated politics from the decline of the Liberal Party in the 1920s until the Labour Party established its hegemony in the 1970s. This alliance was underpinned by British patriotism – 'for King or Queen and country' – and the two world wars. Most Church of Scotland ministers preached a gospel of British patriotism, expressed through social and national duty, and loyalty to the crown. This was annually reinforced by outdoor remembrance services at war memorials up and down the country, which were accompanied by parades, flags and the wearing of military honours. These events were attended by communities in general rather than just congregational members, and showed the national Church ethos at work in a markedly monarchical fashion.

During and after World War Two, the united Church of Scotland also played a positive part in peace and reconstruction initiatives nationally and internationally, including the world-wide ecumenical movement. At home, the Church Extension scheme provided much needed community support in hundreds of new housing schemes, and Church-run social services for children and the elderly expanded nationally. Sunday Schools and youth organizations were bulging at the seams. By the mid-1950s over three million of the adult population were connected with the Church of Scotland.

The thinking of the General Assembly through these years was wide ranging and ready to debate constructively all aspects of modern life, including Scottish Home Rule. In terms of numbers alone, but also in endeavour, this was a national Church. What many at the time, and since, did not realize was how recent many of these developments actually were. The 1929 Church of Scotland is still less than a century old, and its 1950s heyday was to prove dramatically short-lived.

The decline of the Church of Scotland as a national institution began in the 1960s. At first the drop in formal membership was steady rather than alarming. But counting attendance at occasional communion services as membership concealed a much larger-scale trend towards a nominal rather than active Church connection. Being semi-detached may have been an attitude of mind in earlier decades, but it was normally unexpressed because prevailing social attitudes favoured formal religion. The difference from the 1960s on was that nominal attachment became respectable in Scottish society, quickly establishing itself as the natural default position. Within a generation nominal attachment was being replaced by indifference.

From the 1970s numerical decline set in at a remorseless rate. By 2014 the genuinely active and committed membership of the Church of Scotland will barely exceed 200,000 adults, with the numbers of children and young people involved in congregational education comprising a tenth of that number. Participation in the Roman Catholic Church, measured through attendance at mass, held up much more strongly in the late twentieth century, but is now declining steadily. Ironically the normalization of Catholicism within Scottish society is contributing to this decline, by lessening differences between those brought up as Roman Catholics and the majority's detachment from institutional religion. Only Polish immigration slowed the decline in Catholic attendance, in the same way that other world religions in Scotland have been strengthened by the desire of immigrants to sustain their identity through religion.

The phenomenon of religious decline is described by sociologists as 'secularization'. Scotland's recent experience is one of the most rapid processes of secularization for which there is recorded evidence. This seems to mirror the speed with which industrialization and urbanization changed Scotland in the early nineteenth century, and created the conditions for mass religion in the first place. Secularization is a vital clue to understanding how and why Scotland has changed.

Participation in organized religion and religious belief are not the same thing. Many people who are not active in, or even related to, church structures still profess belief in God, though such attitudes are much harder to quantify or assess. Yet the fact that a majority of people in Scotland still describe themselves as having some form of religious belief suggests that the reasons for church decline may not be primarily religious. Nor are they political. The root causes are social and ethical.

Going back to the 1960s and 1970s (1960s trends lagged behind in socially conservative Scotland), it is clear that disaffection with church institutions began with ethical issues, particularly sexual ethics. Contraception, relationships outside marriage, abortion, and later homosexuality were the fault lines extending into disputes about censorship, public expression, popular culture and the media. Individualism and a degree of optimism were in the air, but by and large the institutional churches continued to depict a fallible, sinful world in constant need of official religious instruction. In some cases this was converted into a condemnatory crusade against 'the permissive society'. Individual choice was viewed as selfish and threatening to social order, as well as to the traditional Christian morality on which it depended.

Though there were vocal critics of the Churches in the media and the arts, far more significant was a widespread shift in attitude affecting those inside and outside the Churches. People were no longer willing to be told what to think on such matters, while within families younger people began to strongly resist the idea that they should simply conform to previous expectations. The scale of this shift only gradually became evident, because it was not led by public campaigns or policies, but by people voting with their feet. The Churches' attempt to man the barricades of official British morality seem in retrospect like King Canute commanding the tide to turn back.

Moreover, while a church critique of selfish individualism might seem appropriate to Christianity, the 1960s shifts were not simplistically individualistic. Idealism and spirituality were also in evidence with peace movements, anti-nuclear campaigns, aid to the developing world, and a general disillusion with the politics of Empire and exploitation. With some notable exceptions, such as the Iona Community in Scotland and Roman Catholic liberation theology in South America, the church institutions missed the prophetic boat on this front as well. They continued to be perceived in Scotland as part of the established power structures, representing vested interests and the old order.

As the scale of these challenges became apparent, there was no lack of debate within the institutional Churches, along with a growing realization of the need for radical change. The Second Vatican Council instigated a wave of changes in Catholicism aimed at making participation more meaningful for all. Successive General Assemblies debated blueprints for change across the Church of Scotland. The Scottish Churches Council, based at the newly created Scottish Churches House in Dunblane, pointed to the international ecumenical movement as both an inspiration and a framework for radical re-engagement with modern societies.

But while local churches undertook many creative initiatives in their own communities, the overall structures remained stubbornly resistant to radical change. This was because they could not, or would not, accommodate the challenge to central control which was implicit in these change agendas. Consequently no effective or widely owned reform processes were put in place. Top-down tinkering was the order of the day.

When decline continued through the 1980s and 1990s, the Churches' financial resources came under pressure, and a defensive reaction began. Even as a brief burst of millennial hope and celebration occurred around 2000, centralizing power structures were being strengthened. The ecumenical organizations formed in the late twentieth century were brought under tighter denominational control, and many shared initiatives – such as Scottish Churches House – were shut down on the grounds of cost.

Internal debate also became subject to increasing controls in both the major church traditions as the new century got underway. In Roman Catholicism the hierarchy provided the readily available instrument, and a sophisticated press and media operation began to highlight a tiny number of official voices vigorously promoting conservative views. The Church of Scotland turned to secular management systems to quell the Presbyterian love of debate in favour of 'official lines' on contentious issues such as same sex relationships. The General Assembly was disempowered by managerial complexity, while the work of the Church as a national institution became the domain of a professional administration intent on institutional survival.

Fear of the future became the underlying psychological driver, at the same time as political change set the agenda for Scottish society, and the new Parliament was seen as the instrument of reform rather than any Church. Ecclesiastical ostriches multiplied even as the Churches visibly shrank. Where did all this leave the question of a national Church?

It is arguable that for a period after the Scottish Parliament was re-established in 1999, the Roman Catholic Church leadership aspired to become the *de facto* national Church in a changed Scotland. This became possible because of slower decline and the acceptance of Catholicism, after generations of discrimination and sectarianism, into the mainstream of Scottish society. Having traditionally been a bulwark of the Labour Party vote, Catholics were now as likely to vote SNP as everyone else, and a flirtation ensued between the hierarchy and the nationalist leadership, boosted by a first full official papal visit to Scotland in 2010.

However, relations soon soured over ethical questions such as same sex marriage. It also became clear that the Church's hardline and high-profile media strategy was disconnected from the views of many Catholics. These contradictions blew up in dramatic fashion at the start of 2013, when Scotland's high-profile Roman Catholic leader, Cardinal Keith O'Brien, resigned after admitting 'inappropriate' behaviour. Disastrously for the Cardinal, whose public pronouncements had been vehemently anti-gay, this behaviour concerned relationships with young priests and priests in training. The embarrassment was international as the Cardinal was about to depart for the conclave in Rome to elect a new Pope, at which he would have been the only British representative. Apart from the personal tragedies involved, the whole approach of the Scottish Catholic Church to Scottish public life was left in ruins, after a high point that had been more apparent than real.

As for the Protestant Church of Scotland, it remained the national form of religion under the 1921 Act, and underpinned by the guarantees about religion in the Treaty of Union. Any negotiation for independence or further political autonomy, subsequent to the 2014 Referendum, may amend the effects of the Treaty through legislation at Westminster, but is unlikely to annul the 1707 Union which is the basis of so much shared legislation through recent centuries. An independent Scottish Parliament, in contrast to a devolved Parliament, would however be empowered to make constitutional changes for Scotland.

In that situation, the Scottish Parliament might exclude the Church of Scotland, and religious institutions in general, from any special place in the constitution. Ironically this would be made easier by the Church of Scotland's standoffish relationship with the monarchy and civil government: the Queen can continue seamlessly to play her part without the Church of Scotland. Alternatively, a new Scottish government might wish to allow present arrangements to continue as a historic custom or courtesy, politely observed to decreasing effect.

Given this background, it was unsurprising to observe the 2013 Church of Scotland General Assembly calling for future monarchs to undergo a separate Scottish coronation, organized by the Church of Scotland though with ecumenical representation. The General Assembly had consistently favoured devolution, apart from one notorious vote on the 1979 proposals, when members were swayed against settled policy by the argument that the proposals for a Scottish Assembly were flawed. But having been silent on the independence issue so far, the 2013 coronation proposal was a clear pitch to retain influence and position in any post-independence settlement. The simultaneous call for a draft constitution to be produced before the Referendum, clarifying the future position of the Church of Scotland as an explicitly National Church, plainly showed the Kirk's hand.

The attempt to remain neutral while securing the Church's place whatever the outcome of the independence Referendum, may prove to be a reversion to Unionist type, given the Church's stake in the UK establishment. There is no democratic mandate for pre-Referendum constitution drafting, so the Kirk's claims lie fallow and ignored.

Moreover, it was profoundly paradoxical that the Church should fall back on its attenuated and historically contentious relationship with the British monarchy as a basis for post-independence claims. This may be because there is no basis other than history for the Church of Scotland to continue as a national Church. It is no longer a lead or leading national body, and the parish system has already been subverted by the Church itself due to dwindling finances and clergy numbers. The idea that either the monarch, or the Scottish Government, would pay special attention to the Church's urgings seemed to hark back to previous centuries.

The recent strategies pursued in national life by both the Church of Scotland and the Roman Catholic Church give the impression of organizations more concerned with their own powers and influence than with spiritual matters. At times they also seem wholly distracted by internal matters and focused above all on asserting internal control. More critically the Churches appear to many in Scottish society to have lost the moral initiative, after centuries in which their Christian teaching confidently shaped morality, public and private.

# 4

# Statehood and Ethics

Politics and morality can be a combustible combination, yet they are inextricably linked. The two great British exponents of a politics driven by moral belief were Margaret Thatcher and Tony Blair. Both felt instinctively that Scotland was fertile ground for their moral approaches, but both came to be comprehensively rejected by the Scottish electorate.

To what extent is the movement for political autonomy in Scotland connected with ethical issues, and how do these relate to the different options for statehood?

Moral choices involve responsibility but also freedom. Without the capacity to act or at least influence events, there can be no ethical effect. Consequently the form that political autonomy takes in Scotland directly shapes the potential moral outcomes.

On issues of personal morality, family relationships and crime, the Scottish Parliament is already the defining legislature. The capacity of Parliament is enhanced and guided by the existence of Scots Law, a distinctive and centuries-old legal system which is closer in ethos to Continental traditions than to English Common Law. Recent arguments concerning the role of the UK Supreme Court, and the relationship between the UK and the European Court of Justice, show how jealously the rights of different legal jurisdictions are guarded, even in a period when there is a growing body of international law. The existence of the Parliament greatly strengthens Scots Law, while also benefiting from its traditions and disciplines.

The Scottish Parliament and its committee system have proved effective in delivering improvements to areas of civil and criminal law. The process allows for input from interested parties and a healthy level of scrutiny before draft Bills are finalized. Some measures such as those tackling the vexed problem of sectarianism in Scottish football have appeared more rushed and problematic. Potential legislation on same sex marriage remains controversial, yet the existence of the Parliament will enable this to be debated in a way that reflects mixed views in Scottish society, but also the thirst for progressive change and equality.

Parliament in Edinburgh has also vigorously debated 'the right to die', gender and equality issues, the rights of carers, environmental concerns such as genetically modified crops and fracking, and social justice, without necessarily enacting fresh legislation. Overall the Scottish Parliament has proved itself a strong national forum for debating issues of moral and social as well as political concern. Abortion law remains reserved to Westminster on the grounds that there is a need for a UK-wide consistency, though in fact Northern Ireland already has a different and much more restrictive legal framework.

In matters of tax and social security the Scottish Parliament has little power or influence. The austerity measures imposed by the Westminster coalition government in the wake of the global financial crisis impacted directly on Scots, not least the vulnerable, but Edinburgh could only tinker at the edges. This comes back to the Parliament's overall lack of economic powers. As its income derives from a block grant from Westminster which is directly related to its expenditure choices, the vital interface between economic resource and social choice is stymied in Scotland. Without the capacity to choose there cannot be a moral effect.

There is a political consensus in Scotland that the powers of the Scottish Parliament need to be increased to address this gap between democratic mandate and expenditure choices. Advocates of 'devolution max' argue that more economic powers, such as the raising and spending of income tax, could be devolved without further constitutional change. However, creating two different tax regimes might stretch political cohesion to breaking point. Could devolution max ever provide sufficient powers for the smaller partner in the Union to follow a different path? What would happen if governments in the respective capitals were diametrically opposed in their use of economic instruments for political aims?

The same questions apply to environmental policy where the Scottish Government has set out to be a model of progressive policy change, in line with international agreements. However, without economic powers the Parliament's environmental ambitions are considerably restricted since tax, pricing and demand all play their part in effecting behavioural change. Where Parliament has relevant powers, such as the regulation of land management and ownership, it has acted, but the big levers of environmental change are beyond its grasp.

There is an interesting comparison to be made with the Parliament's success in matters of public health, such as the ban on smoking in public places. Here the Parliament's powers and the Scottish Government's role in managing the Health Service come together to good effect. At the time of writing, similar efforts in relation to alcohol pricing are meeting stiff legal resistance from the drinks industry, but again Parliament is using its existing powers to address a severe social problem.

In both instances the approach is not moralistic but social, yet the resulting improvements enable personal moral choices and well-being. It has been argued that this kind of legislation is patronizing, controlling and a denial of economic freedom. But that ignores the failure of individual choice to tackle the blights of smoking, and alcohol and drug addiction in Scotland, along with their devastating consequences for everyone, not just the immediate consumers. Once again, however, these issues link back to economic performance, since the main driver of poor health and addiction is poverty. Greater social justice, based on fairer distribution of wealth as well as its production, could raise the bar for a whole society. But only if that society is sufficiently self-governing, and there is public support for change.

The case for maximum political autonomy, including independence, is that it enables these different areas of public policy to be more fully integrated in a way that meets Scottish needs, and so enhances potential across a whole society. The argument against this is that these matters involve international interdependence and that the UK is better able to address them on Scotland's behalf, while allowing for devolution of some powers to the Scottish level.

Here pragmatism and morality mingle. If the moral benefit of autonomy is greater for the people of Scotland as a whole, then is there a moral obligation to pursue this course? But if the practical effects of independence could on balance reduce potential improvements, then pragmatically should it be avoided at all costs? Is this a case of moral aspiration versus practical prudence? Yet weighing the consequences of such complex changes seems in itself an almost impossible task. In the end there is a balance of risk and opportunities which may be tipped by fear or desire, by freedom and faith, as much as a would-be rational calculation.

Both sides of the ethical argument concern international frameworks. As global interdependence grows these become ever more important. Does this in itself have moral implications for political conduct? In particular, is national interest any longer a reliable indicator of human well-being, or even survival? What might be Scotland's future role in these relationships, and the UK's with or without Scotland?

Immigration has become a touchstone issue in contemporary British politics. At the time of writing, the Conservative Party, harried by the UK Independence Party, has moved steadily to the right on immigration, drawing the other parties after it. More restrictions have been imposed by the coalition government in London, despite evidence that immigration is helpful to the economy, good for international trade, and essential to the Higher Education sector.

The reason for hardening public policy is the view that a settled majority of the English electorate resents immigration. This, however, does not apply in Scotland, where the majority view is positive towards immigration. Moreover, Scotland desires population growth for the future. Since devolution came into force in 1999, the Scottish population has begun to grow, through immigration and an increasing birth rate, as well as people living longer.

There may be a wider context to these attitudes. Scotland is historically a nation of immigration and emigration. It does not consequently have an island psychology, but a strong sense of interconnection. The eighteenth-century Scottish Enlightenment was curious about other cultures and respectful of cultural difference, not least because Scottish society was itself culturally diverse. Scottish intellectual life has combined a love of homeland with internationalism since medieval times, and the contemporary cultural scene in Scotland blends internationalism with a strong sense of Scottish identity.

In short, Scotland is an international bridge builder with an appetite for constructive diplomatic engagement and cultural friendship. It seems self-evident that Scottish society has both the desire and the capacity to act in its own right as a small nation, and that this would enable Scotland's distinctive attitudes and ethical choices to be reflected in ways that are not possible within the Union with England.

One international framework within which Scotland could naturally operate is the EU. Whatever the process of admission or re-admission might be, Scotland is already an active European player with its own base in Brussels. Again political attitudes towards the EU diverge in the UK, with an often-surfacing desire in England for an in-out Referendum on EU membership, while in Scotland there is longstanding majority support for membership.

Geographically Scotland is surrounded by small nations including Denmark, Norway, Ireland, Sweden, the Netherlands, Finland and Iceland, who have made a success of either full membership or some form of associate relationship with the EU. Alongside the political and economic dimensions, the EU has strong social and environmental objectives. In addition, one of the EU's founding missions is the resolution of internal conflicts. This then extends to a worldwide contribution as a peacemaker and peacekeeper. Membership of the EU offers a strong counter to the argument that Scotland's international contribution can only be effective within the stronger UK framework.

But Europe is not the only context for Scotland's international engagement. The Scots diaspora is worldwide and, in addition to countries in which a significant number of people claim Scots heritage, there are historic trading and cultural links with the Middle and Far East, Africa, the Pacific, India, Latin America and the Caribbean. Unlike the UK as a whole, Scotland has had no opportunity to exercise political or economic influence in any of these regions. Rather, its interest has been in promoting trade, cultural links and international development.

It is questionable whether the current UK project 'to make Britain Great again' is in line with Scotland's social character or in its best interests, even presuming that the project is realizable in contemporary global conditions. The present coalition government seems to be willing to sacrifice equality and social cohesion in favour of economic competitiveness. The Scottish view is that a cohesive society is more successful. This argument, though, is about moral preference as well as self-interest. Equally a different international role for Scotland outside the UK would reflect moral attitudes and preferences. How might such preferences be played out in areas such as terrorism, the global environment, peacekeeping and international aid?

In 1988 Scotland suffered its worst peacetime atrocity when a Pan Am flight was brought down at Lockerbie by a terrorist bomb. Continuing doubts about the investigation and the conviction of Abdelbaset al-Megrahi as the Lockerbie bomber have been described as a stain on Scottish justice. When the Scottish Government released Al-Megrahi on compassionate grounds to return to Libya to die, there was a storm of protest, and Scotland was roundly condemned by governments in Washington and London. Paradoxically this release prevented an appeal hearing which might have led anyway to the quashing of the conviction after Scotland's Criminal Review Board outlined six reasons for believing it to be unsafe.

Many unanswered questions are raised by these events. Were the Scottish police and the judiciary unable to cope with the magnitude of this atrocity? Were they unduly influenced by the Americans in the whole process? Is Lockerbie an example of why Scotland should not try to act independently, or is it a glaring example of how operating at the behest of the international powers can lead to miscarriages of justice and state-sponsored cover-ups?

Realistically, however, could an independent Scotland do any better in such a troubled arena? Would the Scottish propensity towards respect and cultural friendship improve relationships with the Middle East, whose fractious politics lie behind the Lockerbie disaster? The jury remains out on these matters not least because the actual causes of Lockerbie are still unclear 25 years later. Yet would being a moderate, albeit minor, voice in international relations be ethically preferable to trailing in the wake of UK or US foreign policies? Lockerbie poses these dilemmas in an acute form and it is to be hoped, for the sake of grieving relatives, as well as for the international standing of Scottish Law, that some form of closure will be achieved.

The global environmental crisis is as challenging to the international order as terrorism. Scotland aspires to be a leader in environmental good practice, pioneering green energy generation and cutting carbon emissions. At the same time exploiting oil and gas reserves to sustain fuel consumption remains central to the Scottish economy. The unusual conjunction of all these natural resources with a capacity for research and innovation could make Scotland's ambitions credible, as long as financial investment can be attracted.

These developments could take place within a UK framework or in the independence scenario. The UK option might make it easier to attract finance, but equally the focus and prominence of this agenda might be greater as the calling card of a newly independent nation. It is not clear that there is any ethical distinction between these two approaches to the environment.

There is a public policy imperative either way, and it is a political judgement as to which framework may be best suited to advance effective implementation.

That judgement is, however, linked to what role the different political systems would play internationally in EU or UN endeavours to cope with climate change. The ethical agenda locks in here because the effects of climate change are as unequally divided as the world's wealth. Efforts to relieve poverty and promote sustainable development are closely connected.

At the time of writing, expenditure on international aid has been protected by the current UK coalition government, but development aid is often tied to Britain's own economic and political interests. Even peacekeeping operations that have an anti-terrorist purpose could be counted on this reckoning as aid. In a modest way the devolved Scottish Government has encouraged international aid through initiatives such as the Scotland–Malawi partnership. Its activities are closely aligned with the approaches of the charitable aid agencies such as Christian Aid, Oxfam and SCIAF, the Scottish Catholic International Aid Fund.

There is a strong tradition in Scottish society of support for international aid, and Scotland played a very active role in big public campaigns such as the millennium initiative for debt relief – 'Break the Chains' and 'Make Poverty History'. It is likely that an independent Scotland would expand international work for the relief of poverty in line with the established work of the voluntary sector. Public opinion would be strongly opposed to aid being tied to political, economic or military interests. The bias might be in the other direction with the ability to assist in disaster emergencies being a criterion for how an independent Scottish Defence Force might be constructed.

Decisions on war and peace are politically momentous but also the toughest moral choices faced by politicians. In recent decades Britain has gone to war in the Falkland Islands, Kuwait, Iraq, the Balkans, Afghanistan and Libya. Apart from the Falklands War, Britain's forces have been part of some international coalition, usually led by the USA, and in most cases acting without the full support of the UN. Many Scottish politicians have opposed these military interventions.

Scottish public opinion is normally torn between traditional loyalty to the Scottish regiments once deployed, and opposition to the intervention. As a community, Scotland knows the human cost of war and is reluctant to see lives put at risk. In many cases scepticism about longer-term outcomes from the sacrifice involved has also proved well founded. The loss of public trust in Tony Blair as a national leader was strongly connected with the perception that he misled the public on the reasons for the invasion of Iraq in 2003.

This brings into sharp focus the difference between devolution and independence. Decisions on war are the prerogative of the nation state. An independent Scotland would have the power to decide. As Scotland's military capacities would be limited, there would be a bias towards opting out of global military interventions in favour of peacekeeping missions and emergency relief. The use of military force is one of the main ethical questions surrounding Scotland's future political options.

The stakes on this issue are hugely raised by the present location of Britain's independent nuclear deterrent on Scottish soil. 'Independence' in this case may be questionable given the dependence on US technology, but theoretically Britain could launch a devastating nuclear strike from a submarine anywhere in the world, offensively or defensively. Retaliation would come next. The consequences in loss of life and environmental catastrophe seem disproportionate to any political objective. Meanwhile, Scots house this risk on their doorstep, but have no say over location, management or deployment.

The removal of nuclear weapons from Scottish territory, and the potential disabling of Britain's nuclear capacity, is the biggest moral issue in the current independence debate. It raises further questions about Scottish membership of NATO and the financial implications of withdrawal from the UK military. But these aspects are subsidiary to the main choice – nuclear or non-nuclear. The SNP and the Greens have made the removal of nuclear weapons part of their platform for independence, while the other established parties have made Scotland's part in Britain's defence and defence industries a main plank of their campaign to stay British.

But though this choice has huge moral resonance, can it be decided on primarily moral grounds? An underlying desire for 'security' and protection might prevail. The economic case for sharing in UK defence investment could sway some, while a psychology of patriotism and military support might be more widespread in Scotland than is generally conceded. These trends may be longer lasting and more influential than the current period of immediate debate. Again wider considerations of confidence, freedom and fear may play their part.

Choices between the status quo, devolution max and independence have ethical implications because they involve different levels of responsibility. The argument for greater political autonomy brings with it the potential for moral impact as well as greater risk. At the same time it is apparent that the moral calculus does not operate in isolation from other factors. In politics moral choices are wrapped up with pragmatic means and consequences. In addition, morality itself is embedded in society and culture, and strongly influenced by these contexts.

# 5

# Statehood and Culture

Traditionally the two forces that shaped cultural life in Europe were custom and patronage. Custom underpinned the seasonal celebrations and rites of passage around which song, music, story, dance and folk drama clustered. Patronage was an attribute of power, whether exercised by secular rulers or religious institutions. They employed artistic skills to reinforce their status and values, often acting in alliance with each other.

Gradually education also became an influence as the idea took root that there was a realm of knowledge, derived originally from the classical world, that conferred value in its own right. From this development a new secular priesthood of learning emerged to compete with monarchs or priests. Culture became in its own way powerful and an object of distrust, control or suppression.

Competing influences gave rise to the problematic distinction between 'high' and 'low' culture. This may have more to do with 'who pays' than with any genuinely aesthetic judgement. If an art form such as folk song could be practised without patronage from an economic or learned elite, then it was classified as popular art. By contrast, an art form that required financial support from a patron, because of its complex production requirements, has often claimed the status of high art.

Such distinctions passed over into the industrial era. That which was mass produced and popular became low art, while high art forms such as classical music positioned themselves as select activities for those aspiring to higher cultural values. While aristocratic and religious patronage continued, education

was now expanding its influence both through formal school-
ing and voluntary cultural activities. One example of this was
the arts and crafts movement which tried to reach across the
divide to give the folk arts back to the working classes.

During World War Two the British government became
interested in the arts as a way of raising morale and boosting
national coherence. Was culture not part of what made Britain
British, and therefore part of what people were fighting for?
These wartime motivations passed into postwar reconstruction.
The arts could contribute to the tone of the nation, socially and
educationally. Under the guidance of John Maynard Keynes,
the Labour government set up the first Arts Council of Great
Britain in 1947, as a successor to the wartime Committee for
the Encouragement of Music and the Arts.

At the time no one considered the impact on popular culture,
which was seen as something apart, or the relationship between
these subsided activities and self-supporting art such as com-
mercial theatre or amateur music. The presumption was that
what the Arts Council supported needed subsidy because of its
special aesthetic value. The danger of this approach was that
subsidy would come to define what was aesthetically valuable.
In 1948 the Local Government Act empowered local authorities to spend a sixpenny rate on 'entertainment and the arts'.

In 1947 the Edinburgh International Festival was founded
with the support of the British Council, who wished to foster
European reconstruction. Edinburgh was seen as a European
city, and a sort of capital which was not directly embroiled in
the political controversies surrounding the peace settlements.
Though the Festival was funded directly from London until
1952, the Arts Council quickly set up its own Scottish Committee. The Scottish local authorities too were empowered to spend
a fourpence halfpenny rate on entertainment and the arts – a
slightly more prudent allocation than England's sixpence.

The Scottish Committee of the Arts Council followed UK
cultural policies and applied them to Scotland. The focus was
on 'improving' Scottish cultural life, rather than defining a Scottish cultural programme worthy of support. When the Scottish

Committee wished to establish a ballet company, they ignored Glasgow's 'Celtic Ballet', and invited Western Theatre Ballet to move from Bristol to Glasgow. Even in 1970 the Arts Council considered making Bristol's Prospect Theatre Company a Scottish National Theatre by transplanting them to Edinburgh.

These discussions were of their time, but they do reveal the extent to which the new regime of state patronage viewed culture as a tap to be turned on and off, showering people with good things regardless of social context or community traditions. This was unsurprising from the Arts Council which was staffed by 'artistic experts' advising the great and the good. It is more puzzling that local authorities tended to fall in with the new policies, without considering the existing cultural interests and activities of their electorates.

The arts were seen as something different, superior to local social customs and entertainment, and thus culturally improving. Such high arts had their own standards which were grudgingly supported by local authorities in a deferential and largely unconsidered fashion. There was little or no attempt to relate arts funding to other 'cultural' services such as libraries, museums and education.

This underlying approach became explicit in the attempt of the Arts Council to distinguish between 'play-goers' and 'theatre-goers'. The former were engaging in serious artistic activity worthy of state patronage; the latter were indulging in popular entertainment. In 1961, the Scottish Committee instituted a bonus scheme for 'plays of good quality' to counter what they saw as an inclination on the part of Scottish theatres to put on popular shows drawing large audiences of 'theatre-goers'. Given the longstanding tradition of popular theatre in Scotland, this approach reeks of class bias. Also the 'crime' of full theatres seems a little bizarre given later trends. Yet the Arts Council would have been horrified by such an accusation: they were applying their normal 'independent' aesthetic values.

The Arts Council's policies depended on increasing public 'subsidy', which was the new way of describing patronage, at local and national levels. But why had the economic basis of cultural activity become so weak in postwar Scotland? Music, theatre, the visual arts and literature had all flourished in Victorian and Edwardian Scotland with a mixture of popular appeal and patronage. But state subsidy now appeared to be working consciously against economic trends, such as the appeal of Hollywood movies, on the grounds that they were culturally deficient or even harmful. Meanwhile the traditional forms of popular entertainment moved seamlessly into radio and television. Folk music took to the airwaves, and variety acts adapted to the small screen.

In 1967 the Scottish Committee of the Arts Council of Great Britain became the Scottish Arts Council (SAC). Though endowed with a higher profile and more freedom of action, the SAC remained part of the UK Arts Council, reporting to Parliament through the UK Office of Arts and Libraries. In 1994 the SAC became a responsibility of the Scottish Office. These arrangements were designed to protect the 'arm's length' principle, separating politicians from decisions about the funding of culture.

This was certainly successful since between 1967 and the devolution vote in 1997, there seems to have been no parliamentary question about the SAC, and no occasion on which they appeared before a parliamentary committee to give evidence. The first example of this actually occurred between the 1997 vote and the opening of the Scottish Parliament, when the Scottish Select Committee at Westminster grilled the SAC Chair and Director about the withdrawal of funding from Wildcat Theatre Company. The SAC was taken aback by the strength of hostile questioning on this issue.

The absence of democratic debate over the publicly subsidized arts in Scotland is remarkable given the turbulence and controversy that beset arts organizations throughout the 1960s and 1970s. A revolution was underway in attitudes to class, sexual morality and censorship, and in the part played by explicit political debate in culture. These debates took place in the media with an unhealthy divide between the debunkers of the popular press and the often uncritical advocacy of broadsheet commentators, who were in turn closely connected with the arts sector. By and large the democratic process steered clear of such controversial and little understood issues.

None the less, despite the relatively protected position of the decision-makers, public debate about the rights and wrongs of funding decisions had begun. Arts organizations responded to social and political change by diversifying to include political theatre, community arts, and arts in education. Later, folk or traditional arts, and ethnic minority cultures, would be added to the mix, often to the horror of those who felt that classical music, ballet and opera should remain the priorities. In fact, even within an expanding funding pot, the conventional high arts continued to dominate financially.

Scottish identity had been an issue in the 1940s when the new arts institutions were taking shape. But by and large the professionalization of culture in the 1950s and 1960s took priority over such matters. The priority was to establish a support structure for the modern arts. Identity or social function were seen as subsidiary to the essential role of art which transcended mere cultural limitations.

It was therefore very troubling for the SAC when identity politics flared up in the 1970s and 1980s. While arts administrators claimed neutrality and expertise, artists in all forms were actively engaged with the political pressures, even when their creative responses were not explicitly political. The case of 7:84 Theatre is instructive as the SAC recognized its theatrical importance in the 1970s, but then withdrew support in the face of government disapproval in the 1980s, while still trying to justify its actions on 'artistic' grounds. 7:84 England had already lost state funding due to its outright support for the National Miners' Strike, leaving the SAC between the rock of artistic distrust and the hard place of paymaster disapproval. The paradox of a Conservative government with no democratic mandate in Scotland lurks behind these funding decisions.

But something else was happening through these decades that proved to be much more significant in the longer term. Changes in schools, especially the increased provision of music,

art and drama specialists, fed the expansion of higher education through universities, art colleges and the Royal Scottish
Academy of Music and Drama. A new generation of Scottish
teachers and artists emerged for whom the contemporary arts
were part of their social and cultural identity. This new wave
also represented a much wider spectrum of society than the
middle class and often anglified specialists of the postwar era.
The gap between the subsidized contemporary arts and Scottish
society narrowed, leading to a creative boom as local, national
and international influences mixed, competed and sometimes
clashed.

These developments also fuelled the dramatic changes of the
1980s. The Referendum of 1979, and the onset of Margaret
Thatcher's reign, politicized artistic practice in Scotland as a
whole. Against a background of political and social frustra-
tion, cultural participation became an expression of citizenship – a declaration of social and political values – even when
the artistic content was not explicitly political. As democracy
failed to make a difference, the arts became an alternative form
of resistance.

Behind the high-profile fireworks was a growing cultural
confidence, which both harnessed the contemporary arts to
Scottish perspectives and in some cases brought artistic innovation to bear on specifically Scottish subjects. The publication
of Alasdair Gray's influential novel *Lanark* in 1982 is a bench-
mark because it makes the representation of modern Scottish
society part of its theme. Could Glasgow be said to truly exist
as a city until it is given an imaginative expression and identity?
The novel is also the story of a young working-class Glaswe-
gian who goes to art college and tries to apply artistic values
to his society by painting murals in churches. In a sense this
is Alasdair Gray's own journey as an artist and official city
painter during the long period in which his novel was taking
shape.

On another level, *Lanark* is a dystopian satire and fantasy
which comments ironically on the realistic strands of the narrative. This has echoes of Orwell's *1984*, but speaks in Alasdair

Gray's distinctive voice. His defining work is not only a literary achievement, but a successful integration of aesthetic ambition with Scottish social consciousness. Moreover, the success of *Lanark* heralded the increasing internationalization of Scotland's cultural scene.

The impact of Scotland's home-grown artists helped change the institutional landscape as well. In 1992 the 'Charter for the Arts in Scotland' brought the SAC, the local authorities, and the Scottish Museums' Council together in the largest ever public consultation on arts provision. The outcome demonstrated widespread support for all kinds of cultural activity along with a desire for further development. There was also a public appetite for more Scottish cultural products, including drama and the folk arts.

As if on cue, in 1995 the National Lottery doubled the SAC's financial resources. But the purposes of arts funding had also widened to include economic, social and educational benefits along with artistic criteria. Potential beneficiaries increased exponentially, finally proving that the contemporary arts were now thoroughly embedded in Scottish aspirations. Every part of Scotland, socially and geographically, was to some degree signed up to what had been judged only a generation before as 'not for the likes of us'.

The opening of the restored Scottish Parliament in 1999 was greeted with enthusiasm by the artistic community. Both the initial inauguration ceremony and the subsequent inauguration of the parliament building at Holyrood had a strong cultural bedrock, with renditions of Robert Burns's 'A Man's a Man for A' That' and a specially commissioned poem by the Scottish Makar or national poet, Edwin Morgan. However, the first two parliamentary sessions of 1999–2003 and 2003–7 proved an uncomfortable period for politicians and cultural activists alike.

One early positive development was an enquiry by the new Parliament's culture committee into Scotland's national performing arts companies. This achieved the first democratic scrutiny into the possibility of a Scottish National Theatre, reviewing its potential forms and drawbacks, while questioning the factors that had frustrated its emergence. The Committee elicited the first positive proposal from the existing theatre companies as to how such a new entity might operate. This enquiry proved to be the critical first step towards the successful establishment of the National Theatre for Scotland in 2003, with its non-building-based collaborative remit.

The first Scottish Executive (not yet government) led by Donald Dewar moved quickly to produce a cultural policy, 'Remembering the Past; Creating the Future'. This was somewhat rushed and omitted to mention literature, but was none the less a constructive starting point. However, it soon became apparent that the politicians, though keen to put their stamp on cultural policy, had no more idea how to connect the newfound democratic accountability with the arts than the cultural aficionados. Politicians slid into an unanalysed emphasis on economic and social benefits while the cultural mafia grew distrustful.

On St Andrew's Day 2004 the then First Minister Jack McConnell gave a keynote speech at the Royal Scottish Academy of Music and Drama in Glasgow, announcing arts for all as the next great endeavour for Scottish public life. He also proposed a Cultural Commission chaired by James Boyle, who resigned as Chair of the SAC to lead on this wider vision.

Despite a generally rocky ride for the Commission, whose aims were diffuse and lacked procedural rigour, its final report did set out a sweeping vision for change. Among its most important recommendations was the definition by law of cultural rights for all citizens, backed up by locally defined and applied 'cultural entitlements'. The citizens of Scotland had not been engaged with this new 'charter' process, but it appeared to set their participation in the arts on a wholly new footing. Citizenship and culture were to be joined at the hip by law.

But neither government nor the political parties were convinced. The Scottish Executive came forward with its own policy, 'Scotland's Culture', and proceeded to consult on a draft Culture Bill. In this draft the Executive's determination to control the decisions of its proposed new cultural agency, Creative Scotland, was exposed to hostile scrutiny. So was the muddle of 'cultural entitlements' in the Executive's version, which had no defined cultural purpose and to which no one was actually entitled. So cultural politics limped into the third Scottish Election of 2007 in which the Labour–Liberal Democrat Coalition was voted out in favour of the first minority SNP administration.

The new SNP government moved swiftly to establish a set of national objectives by which all policies should be measured. These were focused on economic well-being, social justice and environmental improvement. Culture did not feature in its own right, yet the administration brought forward a 'Creative Scotland Bill', picking up from the previous regime's desire to merge the SAC and Scottish Screen into one unified quango. The language of 'cultural entitlement' was abandoned. Vigorous debate on aims and definitions followed, not least on the implications of adding 'creative industries' to the new body's responsibilities. But at the last gasp a procedural confusion regarding new resources for the wider remit led to the Bill's defeat in Parliament, and the resignation of Linda Fabiani, the Culture Minister.

Finally a redrafted measure was passed in 2010 as part of a Public Services Reform Bill. The purposes of Creative Scotland were now defined as supporting quality and excellence; promoting understanding, appreciation and enjoyment of the arts and culture; encouraging as many people as possible to participate in the arts and culture; and realizing the value and benefits (in particular the national and international value and benefits) of the arts and culture. These were broadly comparable to earlier versions with slightly more emphasis on 'national and international'.

In the new Bill, there was also a tighter definition of responsibility for creative industries, relating only to those activities with a primary focus on 'the application of creative skills'. One clear addition, however, was 'encouraging and supporting artistic and other creative endeavours which contribute to an understanding of Scotland's national culture in its broad sense as a way of life', which seems a clear direction for inclusion of the traditional arts.

After this long drawn-out agony, during which the SAC had been left neither live nor wholly dead, the cultural community was by and large relieved to see the matter resolved. Unfortunately, the start-up process for the new agency proved contentious, and when the new Board commenced work it found that an interim body had already appointed the new-broom senior executive team. But, after only 18 months and a high-profile spat with leading artists, the head of the executive team resigned.

In an atmosphere of crisis, the Board had to take control and begin a series of reforms, seeking to bridge the gap between Creative Scotland's original sweeping rhetoric and the realities of the existing cultural map. This process remains ongoing, but Creative Scotland's honeymoon period of media goodwill and budgetary plenty had come to an uncomfortably spectacular end. Fortunately, most artists and arts organizations simply got on with the job of keeping the show on the road.

The Creative Scotland debacle hogged the creative limelight for a time. But meanwhile other important changes were taking place. The Scottish Broadcasting Commission, chaired by Blair Jenkins, set out a coherent vision for an integrated broadcasting sector, regulated by the Scottish Parliament. Broadcasting had been reserved to Westminster precisely because the broadcasters, especially the BBC, were seen to define the UK. The Commission proposed a Scottish version of the BBC, but realistically such a body could only be established by a Scottish Parliament with increased powers or by an independent Scotland.

In education, however, the existing Parliament did have the necessary devolved powers. A reform process, Curriculum for Excellence, commanded cross-party support and continued from one administration to another. At the core of the reform is the humane value of confident, creative individuals contributing effectively to society in the round. There is a strong tradition of generalist thinking in this ethos, which is rooted in the eighteenth-century Scottish Enlightenment. The Enlightenment thinkers had a strong sense of social context, and emphasized the purpose of specialist knowledge in forming a balanced 'science' of human nature – in the round.

Curriculum for Excellence seeks to provide a framework of values and a methodology for learning, rather than prescribed content. It puts the why and how of learning above the what. None the less, much heat has been generated by the 'what' question. Though the whole process has a distinct Scottish context and character, some pushed also for specific Scottish cultural content, which had historically been underplayed in previous frameworks. On St Andrews Day 2005, the Literature Forum for Scotland petitioned Parliament for recognition of the right of all Scottish citizens to learn something of the country's literature, languages and history.

Though some teachers decried this campaign as 'parochial' or unduly prescriptive, the petition received widespread public support and politicians of all parties were shifting their ground away from a longstanding deference to the educational establishment. By the time a majority SNP administration took power in 2011, steps were underway to provide Scottish cultural resources that at least levelled the field of choice for educators. After all, 'British' or English literature remained compulsory. Yet in instituting these changes the official structures were following change rather than leading. Public interest in Scottish history and culture continued to grow through this period despite, and not because of, the vagaries of policymaking or political positioning.

How can such a process of cultural change be defined? Though connected with politics and education it has its own dynamic. This may have more to do with globalization than nationalism in itself. It is possible both to embrace the positive potential of globalization – such as concerted action against climate change – while at the same time seeing an increased need to foster local environments and diversity. That also explains why the renewed interest in Scottish culture is strongly internationalist and outward-looking rather than reactionary or defensive.

This nascent confidence feeds back in turn into education. Children's learning begins with their immediate environment, and then on the basis of this experience reaches out by analogy and extension to understand other environments and ways of thinking. Some grounding of local culture is vital if people are to grow in understanding on the basis of self-critical awareness. This model will value their own cultural diversity while avoiding either chauvinism or self-denigration.

Yet this uneasy tension between aggressive assertion and low self-esteem is exactly what dogged Scotland, culturally and psychologically, for much of the twentieth century. A lack of grounded self-understanding led many middle-class Scots to look down on their society and culture, without ever exploring their actual heritage. Many working-class communities by contrast remained loyal to local custom and language, but felt themselves marginalized and devalued. This was because their traditions were rarely acknowledged in the wider public realm and were actively discouraged, or even suppressed, at school.

The turnaround sought by Curriculum for Excellence is founded on giving young Scots both the skills and the confidence to actively appropriate cultural processes and content to make their own choices, and so shape the future. Beyond the 2014 Referendum, whatever its outcome, the future lies with the rising generations whose capacities and positive attitudes have long overtaken the stereotypes of dour and suppressed Scots, which were once a staple of popular culture. Perhaps Ian Rankin's Inspector Rebus represents a last late flowering of a Scots archetype which is bowing out.

Religion has also played its ambiguous cultural part as previously described. For many twentieth-century Scots faith remained an expression of distinctive cultural identity. Religion formed and reinforced cultural cohesion. This was true for Western Isles Presbyterians resistant to any dilution of social character in Gaelic-speaking communities; for urban working-class Roman Catholics keeping their solidarity alive; and for otherwise secularized Scots whose cultural identity continued to be vested in the Orange Order. But as the century progressed, and religious institutions failed to address huge social and intellectual changes, these influences appeared culturally defensive and ingrown. Consequently the move towards more outward-looking confidence has often tended to discard religion, or at least its organized forms, as a cultural hindrance.

Yet not all sections of Scottish society have shared equally in the positive cultural narrative. Huge inequalities continue, and in some communities that are still beset by multiple deprivation, the remnants of organized religion and locally based cultural projects are the only organizations left trying to motivate community-owned change. What might greater independence culturally or socially mean in these communities?

Political autonomy could be seen as the logical extension of growing cultural confidence. Equally one might argue that culture can continue to grow in strength within the existing constitutional frameworks. Independence would, however, provide the Scottish Parliament with vital broadcasting powers. Also, culture would be on the frontline of an independent Scotland's international relations, leading to a step change in the kind of internationalization that is already underway. There is at least the possibility that an independent Scotland would be more culturally ambitious and outward-looking.

The social impact of cultural change is harder to gauge. Could greater national pride foster greater social confidence? That is surely dependent in its turn on many complex factors beyond one referendum. If the state Scotland is in, is becoming clearer, if only in outline, what kind of society is Scotland now becoming? That is a cultural question, but also one about wider social character and dynamics. It is about the fabric of people's everyday lives in a rapidly changing world.

# 6

# A Moment in Time

Results from the 2011 Census, combined with the Scottish Household Survey, and other research commissioned by the Scottish Government since devolution, provide an unprecedented level of information about the condition of Scottish society at the time of writing – a period of intense national self-scrutiny that will determine much about Scotland's future direction, whatever the outcome of the Referendum in 2014. Change continues apace and even since 2011 there has been a shift, for example, in patterns of employment, as more people take on part-time work – so sustaining overall employment levels through the longest economic depression yet endured by the UK.

The headline message, though, is one of population growth. At 5.3 million in number, those who presently live in Scotland make it more inhabited than at any time since records began. The growth is not just a product of people living longer, but of an increased birth rate and immigration. If this trend continues it will be one of the biggest historic changes in the modern period, which has been dominated by net outward migration, even when the birth rate was much higher. Moreover, many parts of Scotland remain relatively depopulated and, depending on patterns of land use and employment, there could be room for many more people.

Yet the pattern is not uniform. While cities such as Glasgow and Dundee – which were previously losing people – have stemmed the flow, urban areas in Inverclyde and West Dunbartonshire are still declining. While the mainland Highlands are gaining people, not least through the rapid expansion of Inverness as a Highland capital, Argyll and Bute, which encompasses a sixth of Scotland, is both declining and ageing. Is this an island factor? No, because the Western Isles are holding their own and Shetland has gained in numbers. This most basic of all indicators – the movement of people – shows how difficult it is to construct a unified Scottish narrative. There is diversity and regional variation in every set of data.

Economically, Edinburgh and Aberdeen remain the most prosperous areas, but Glasgow has reversed its decline and Dundee is probably Scotland's most enterprising city in terms of culture, bio-tech industries and computer games. But this conceals the persistence of multiple deprivation in localized concentrations. Despite a steady growth in public expenditure through the first devolution decade, social inequality remains stubbornly entrenched with unemployment, poverty, and low educational achievement predictably interlinked.

The same picture is revealed as regards health. Within overall improvements in life expectancy and survival rates from serious illness, there are whole communities where life expectancy, especially among men, is up to 25 per cent lower than the average. At the same time obesity, diabetes and liver disease are on the up among younger people. Drug abuse remains large scale with devastating consequences. By contrast, deaths from HIV/ AIDS are being reduced both by prevention and the development of life-saving treatment.

On the cultural front, the decline of participation in institutional religion is stronger in the east than in the west. The Gaelic heartland is shifting from the Western Isles, where Gaelic is losing its traditional dominance, to the cities where Gaelic medium education is in growing demand. More people feel themselves to be positively engaged with 'the arts', but exclusion on the grounds of cost has also increased. Rural areas that might be considered prosperous on many economic indicators feel themselves to be lacking in cultural provision and handicapped by poor broadband connections.

The Scottish Census of 2011 also tracks shifts in religion, notably an increase from 28% to 37% of the population since 2001 who state 'no religion' as their self-description. There is also an increase in the relatively small proportion of those adhering to a non-Christian faith, from 2 per cent to 3 per cent. The other big movement is a decline in those identifying 'Church of Scotland' as their form of religion, from 42% to 32%.

Interpreting Church of Scotland statistics requires especial care. Since no one pays a subscription, membership criteria are applied in different ways by local congregations. Removal from 'the membership roll' may only happen some years after a person has ceased being actively involved. On the other hand, some people may be actively involved without formally becoming members. The officially cited membership figure for 2012 was 440,000 people, but church attendance figures suggest that less than half these people are active, while children, as previously suggested, may add another 20,000 to the total.

Yet the 2011 Census still logs 1,700,000 people as aligned with the Church of Scotland. What does that mean? The question asked in the Census is 'What religion, religious denomination or body do you belong to?' Though under Christianity there are options for 'Roman Catholic' and 'Other Christian', there is no option marked 'Protestant'. Those who wish to affirm a continuing Protestant social and cultural identity tick 'Church of Scotland'. This could embrace everything from outright sectarianism to an attenuated and secularized version of 'not being Catholic' or, in general terms, 'not being particularly religious'. Many of those ticking the Church of Scotland box have no meaningful relationship with a Church of Scotland congregation, which explains why the gap between the official membership figures and the Census return is so statistically extreme, and even widened between 2001 and 2011.

There is a further direct correlation between this waning yet still significant Protestant identity and secularization. Between 2001 and 2011 the increase in those stating 'no religion' is almost equivalent to the decline in those stating 'Church of

Scotland' as their religion. Roman Catholicism by contrast has remained stable in overall census numbers, and other faiths have increased. When these data are set beside the new 2011 Census information that 62% affirm 'Scottish only' as their 'national identity', in contrast to 18% affirming 'Scottish and British', then a fascinating picture of interrelated trends emerges.

The situation of the Church of Scotland is, to say the least, challenging. On the one hand its residual strengths are based on diminishing social characteristics, demographically and culturally. At the same time it is exceptionally exposed to the growing characteristic of secularization. This throws some light on the puzzling process by which the central administration of the Church of Scotland has itself become more secularized through the influence of charity governance and management. Many church members are disaffected from the central administration, which is finding it increasingly difficult to find representatives willing to serve as unelected appointees on its committees and councils. It is even possible that a charitable body, legally calling itself a church, could cease to operate on primarily spiritual or theological principles, while focusing on its own internal ethos and financial survival. Paradoxically such a trend might work in parallel with a religious retreat from broad-based social engagement to a narrower and more exclusive piety.

The politics of Scotland are equally complex. With four sets of elections – European, UK, Scottish and local – voters behave differently in each context. While the SNP, under First Minister Alex Salmond, have established a position of strength in the Scottish arena, which in turn influences local elections, voters tend to revert to UK-wide parties when voting for Westminster representation. The European elections suffer from the problem of low turnout, though in fact this issue now dogs all the electoral arenas. What seems rarely mentioned by pollsters is that the result of the forthcoming Referendum, and any future ones, may depend most of all on how many of those who do not normally vote would turn out for such a historic decision.

The politicians meanwhile try to sway people with their own versions of a grander narrative. The UK Prime Minister,

Conservative leader David Cameron, espouses a 'make Britain great again' story which justifies austerity on the grounds that it will make the country globally competitive in economic terms, and end a 'something for nothing' dependence culture in British society. Sitting comfortably with this line is UK success at the 2012 Olympic Games, retaining London as a global financial centre at all costs, renewing Britain's independent nuclear deterrent, and continuing to share in both humanitarian and military interventions worldwide, as befits a permanent member of the UN Security Council. What does not fit with the Cameron narrative is further European integration, the 'secession' of Scotland from the UK, or the kind of restrictive immigration policies implemented by the present UK administration.

The Labour Party narrative has been mainly articulated to date by the old guard of Scottish Labour leaders, such as Alastair Darling and Gordon Brown, who achieved UK stature in the recent past. Their argument is that Scotland will be better off and more secure within the UK, and that a future Labour government will underpin a social justice and equality agenda. In effect, however, this approach slews in a negative direction. There is no Labour government, and the main message is that 'Scotland will do worse on its own', which is the Conservative mantra. The same problem afflicts the 'No' campaign as a whole, whose slogan 'Better Together' seems to imply 'because you can't manage on your own'. It is also unclear at this time where Labour is going at UK level, as in many key areas, including benefit reform and immigration, it has failed to construct a clear or appealing alternative to current coalition policies.

The SNP narrative, led by Alex Salmond and Nicola Sturgeon, is that an independent Scotland can be economically successful and a fairer society. This may appear a 'best of both worlds' sell which is inherently hard to believe, yet it is a coherent story that has the added benefit of being positive and even aspirational. To many Scots witnessing the immediate effects of austerity and benefit cuts, it may also seem quite practical.

The SNP narrative underpins the overall Yes campaign which enlists other aspirational agendas including socialism, the environmental movement, anti-nuclear campaigners, and internationalists who do not subscribe to the Cameron vision of the UK. The SNP narrative also encompasses a pro-European attitude and a 'Scotland welcomes the world' ethos that looks and feels different. Perhaps the greatest success of the SNP story is that it is an outward-looking form of nationalism, one that does not define itself against anything else but its own positive vision. The 'social union' with Scotland's fellow UK nations would continue, argue the SNP, and immigration would be encouraged.

The Liberal Democrats, a political party with a long and proud Scottish tradition, have been marginalized in the debate, because their involvement as junior partner with the Conservatives in the current UK government has denied them a distinctive narrative, particularly in Scotland. Yet their longstanding argument is for a federal UK, which could allow for greater devolution of powers and overall constitutional reform, including a federal Parliament in London and further limitations on the powers of the monarchy. A federal UK would also sit more comfortably within the EU. The federal solution is a common-sense narrative with at present no effective champions, and no possibility of practical implementation in the current English political climate. At the time of writing the right-wing UK Independence Party is outpolling the Liberal Democrats in elections south of the border.

Many commentators and some voters are frustrated by the clash of narratives and demand 'facts'. What will be the relationship of an independent Scotland to the EU, or to NATO? What will be the tax regime for business and how will Scotland use the pound sterling as a currency when it is regulated by the Bank of England? Others require answers to constitutional issues such as the role of local government or the place, if any, of the Church of Scotland in the new order.

Parties to the debate, which include two governments and two Parliaments, will go on refining their policies or views on these issues, but the substance will not be decided till after the vote. That is because detailed answers would be the subject of intensive negotiation, and of a continuing political process at Scottish, UK and European levels. In addition, rapidly moving economic and political circumstances could affect the outcomes in unexpected ways.

What, for example, would be the impact if, subsequent to the Referendum on Scottish independence, the UK voted in a referendum to leave the EU? If Scotland voted yes in 2014, would Scots need to have a separate ballot in a 2017 vote on Europe? It seems quite likely that whatever the 2014 decision, Scots will soon be back at the polls again voting on major constitutional change. It is also possible that the outcomes from these 'in principle' decisions might require further ratification from the electorate.

The concept that a single choice based on a set of rational criteria, for and against, will be decisive is flawed. The picture is much more complex and involves how people collectively and individually feel things are changing in the round. That is where the competing stories impact. It is the degree to which they connect with all the other social, economic and cultural factors that will swing things one way or another. And these trends will not be just about one vote, but a longer game. If recent political history teaches anything in Scotland it is that what seemed uncertain and divisive in 1979 became unifying and decisive in 1997, less than 20 years later.

Though much harder to define than political or social trends, psychological and spiritual influences are also at play. The weakness of institutional religion in contemporary Scotland has displaced many conventional aspects of religious faith into culture and politics. Identity, hope, community values, dignity, respect and ethical principles are the stuff of religious discourse, but also figure frequently in the constitutional discussion. The relationship between the public domain and the well-being of individuals, families and communities is the underlying crux of the decisions about what kind of society Scotland aspires to be. Again there is a wider awareness of the dehumanizing force of economic globalization and the desire to foreground other aspects of human value.

There is a concern on all political fronts not to allow the debate to become a matter of identity politics in the narrower sense. Yet the key issue is about how people living in their own places define their coherence and connection. This becomes a question of Scottish identity and its appropriate expression, as well as its relationship to other sources of identity. No party to the debate denies that Scottish identity is fully alive, evolving, and possibly more vigorous than it has ever been. In what way might this sense of identity carry spiritual resonance?

Contemporary understandings of religion and spirituality have been affected by the war between fundamentalism and atheism. Wars tend to distort, and this one is no exception. Unfortunately the battles are not solely intellectual since behind the debate is a worldwide struggle between Western-influenced thinking and a defensive reaction on the part of cultures that see themselves as threatened. Scotland has its own issues with the positive and negative consequences of globalization, but fortunately they do not constitute a literal battlefront.

In this wider global conflict religion has been enlisted in the cause of armed resistance, while 'the war against terror' claims universal humanist values as its justification. This fault line is not confined to Islamic relations with Western societies, since it divides the USA itself where religious fundamentalists defy liberal social norms. India, where the fundamentalist cause is Hindu, is also involved, while in Russia, Christianity rather than secularism claims to be the state's defender against extremism.

But the God who features in these disputes bears little relationship to the mature thinking of any of these faith traditions. In reaction to the rise of science and the prestige of its form of knowledge, fundamentalist religion claims a rival pseudo-scientific certainty for theological creeds. But the language and concepts of religion are not scientific or solely a pre-scientific alternative to causal thinking. They offer a different kind of metaphorical and metaphysical conceiving which is deeply rooted in our minds and emotions. Religious thinking and imagining neither denies nor confirms scientific proofs, though it can be in creative dialogue with them, in the interests of a wider and deeper sense of humanity and its place in the universe.

Militant atheism bypasses the complexities of religious or philosophic thought to target the fundamentalists' concept of an absolutely certain God, whose strict instructions can be depended on to resolve every problem. Having knocked down this straw divinity, the anti-Goddists feel vindicated, while outraged fundamentalists respond by burning books and sometimes professors. The atheist cause is often backed up by making science an alternative form of absolute certainty, but in most cases this is hardly necessary, since the fundamentalist position already defies common sense and admits no common ground for dialogue.

The negative outcome of this strident debate is that both religion and science come to be seen as fixed ideologies, rather than as open modes of thought contributing to our common life. They are deployed as weapons to direct and coerce people, and so become tainted by association, whether with capitalist economies or with terrorism. The fundamentalists have done enormous damage by alienating many of those who need and desire religion in their lives. Dogmatic science also misrepresents the nature of its own open-ended enterprise.

There is a gulf between this conflict-laden scenario and the way in which twentieth-century Scottish writers explored religion, both as a negative institutional influence, and as a source of creative thinking. From Patrick Geddes, Neil Gunn and Naomi Mitchison, to Robin Jenkins, Tessa Ransford and George Mackay Brown, the wordsmiths intertwine identity, spirituality and morality with a vivid sense of the natural and social environments. Respect for the past imbues their creations, but there is also a resolve to tell things as they are, and imagine afresh. The poets, novelists and essayists have delivered a powerful critique of Scottish religion, and generated a spiritual energy around Scotland's self-understanding which is an important part of contemporary culture.

Given such contrasting perspectives on religion, how is the spiritual aspect of the discussion about Scotland's future to be advanced? Does organized religion still have a contribution to make and, if so, what form might that take? If changing lives by building a society founded on human dignity and respect is the core objective, then spirituality has to be addressed, even if the answers may take religion into some uncharted waters.

# 7

# Sin and Salvation

The formative impact of Christianity on Scottish society is bound up with the twin ideas of sin and salvation. Sin covers morally bad actions, and the states of mind or feelings that cause them. In this perspective the human condition is inescapably sinful, and what is required is divine intervention to save people, collectively and individually, from themselves and one another.

Both sin and salvation – the disease and the remedy – raise issues of human freedom. If humanity is inescapably sinful then our condition is predetermined, fated or even cursed. In addition, if divine intervention is required to put things right, then equally human capacity or initiative is limited. Moreover, if some are saved rather than others, is that a question of human choice or God's will?

This is where the Church comes into play in Christian thinking. In the Roman Catholic version, the Church is God's chosen means of helping people move from sinful intent and action to a life inspired and supported by God. Human will or conscience still plays a vital role but needs help. In practice, the requirement of Catholicism is to choose to surrender free choice, in favour of obedience to the Church.

In the Protestant version, as developed in Scotland, the human will is corrupted by sin: only faith can restore our relationship with the divine and make us capable of goodness. Such faith, though, is God's gift, and only some are chosen or predetermined to receive faith. Unfortunately no one can be certain that he or she is chosen or saved, making human life an anxious search for 'signs of assurance'. At the same time being in a state of grace lifts humankind beyond the mere requirements of morality, which could be an elevating and yet dangerous state. Someone might become so assured of their own blessedness that they feel superior to mere morality. Hence James Hogg's classic study of religious delusion, *The Private Memoirs and Confessions of a Justified Sinner*.

In this Protestant version of salvation, the job of the Church is to point people on the right path by preaching God's word as revealed in the Bible. Then the faithful must be guided through self-examination to seek signs of assurance, and led through prayer and self-discipline on a journey of 'sanctification'.

Historically Scotland experienced this emphatic version of Protestantism, inspired by John Calvin, from the sixteenth century onwards. When Roman Catholicism was re-established in the nineteenth and twentieth century, it was also in a strongly puritanical form influenced by post-famine Ireland. This Catholic ethos was as emphatic about sin as the Protestant one, along with the consequent need in Catholicism for absolute obedience to the Church.

At periods of social or political conflict these religious ideas have been agents of change, challenging established authority. Scottish history is full of examples of radical reforming religion. Over the long term, though, such ideas, as applied by the Churches of both traditions, became disempowering. When the Churches were established as dominant institutions, conformity was valued in its own right and Christianity reinforced social norms rather than challenging them. Religion came to define social convention, and this legacy left the Scottish Churches ill-prepared for radical social change.

But there was another underlying psychological effect. Both Christian approaches, Protestant and Catholic in its restored form, eroded the cultural connections between people and place. Both regarded traditional and local culture as tainted with sin, and therefore suspect. In periods of increased mobility the Churches willingly stepped in to provide an alternative form of culture moulded by their beliefs. The links between people, place and ways of life were broken. This process began in Lowland and urban areas, and then in the eighteenth century took hold in the Highlands.

The purpose of these reforming, evangelical changes was to make life more spiritual and ethical. But the net result was to divide existence into separate religious and secular compartments. The Churches might provide a more purified religious experience than older faith traditions, but society became utilitarian and materialistic, not least in its relationship with the natural world.

There was also a direct impact on artistic expression. The growth of Puritanism, in both Protestant and Catholic versions, involved a distrust of the senses, and of what the body might be telling the mind. This constrained dance, drama and the visual arts, and channelled faith expressions into specific forms of literature and music which were encouraged or directly patronized by the Church. The folk arts as a whole were discouraged – and even actively suppressed – until attitudes, in some Churches, mellowed in the late nineteenth and early twentieth centuries. From the mid-nineteenth century on, a wider palette of religious art also crept back, motivated by a conscious attempt to revive pre-Reformation patronage of the arts and crafts.

To explore the psychological and spiritual effects of mainstream Christianity, it is necessary to delve a little deeper into theological ideas and the way they have been applied. This may provide a perspective on how faith is changing in Scottish society, along with some indications for the future.

If God is good and in command of the universe, why do suffering and wrongdoing appear to have a free hand? The twin problems of evil and undeserved pain have dogged Christianity since its inception as an organized religion.

The classical answer to this contradiction is that God, having given his creatures free will, has then to accept the bad consequences of humanity's moral choices along with the good, rather like the prodigal father in the New Testament parable. That, however, cannot really convince, because much of what people suffer is not a direct consequence of their own moral choices. It cannot fairly be described as an outcome of their free will.

Cue a long-running, supplementary Christian explanation. Humankind as a whole, many theologians have argued, is in a 'fallen' or sinful state, ever since the serpent 'tempted' Eve who tempted Adam to make an incorrect moral choice in the Garden of Eden. This story of origins does offer a rationale for social and psychological ills that are beyond individual moral actions, yet it can hardly be stretched to explain loss of life from earthquakes, volcanoes and other 'natural' disasters.

However, the entire notion of a 'fallen state' – a moral genetic blight that afflicts people regardless of personal moral worth – sits strangely with Christ's affirmation of a Creator who loves each part of creation in its own right. It also flatly contradicts Jesus' specific teaching that the sins of the father should not be visited on the children. Humanity as a whole may struggle with inherent moral flaws and difficulties, but these cannot fairly be blamed on human beings individually or collectively.

Over-emphasis on a 'fall' in the Garden of Eden is a side effect of reading sacred texts such as the book of Genesis in the Jewish Scriptures as if they were meant to be literal accounts or scientific explanations. This modern notion is quite foreign to the culture and thinking of those who created, edited and interpreted the biblical Scriptures.

The Adam and Eve story is a classic 'pourquoi' or 'how it came to be' narrative. Such stories tell us how things are, using metaphor and symbol; they are not causal chronologies. The Genesis storytellers are brilliantly analysing the moral and spiritual complexity of humans, who are gifted with a self-consciousness that can tend towards illumination and joy, or towards a destructive lust for power and control.

The role of 'God' in these narratives cannot simplistically be conflated with the divine Creator of the universe. Later editors actually refused to speak or spell out God's name, substituting symbolic letters to represent the 'holy name'. The actions ascribed to 'God' and his motivations are morally ambiguous, throwing humans out of Eden so that they cannot become gods like him. 'God' goes for evening strolls in his garden, and decides at one point to wipe out creation before having second thoughts. The editors give a clear indication that they are using mythic imagery when, between the story of Adam and Eve and that of Noah, they describe 'the sons of God' marrying 'the daughters of men', so giving birth to a race of heroes and giants.

While ascribing an ultimate divine origin to all things, the Genesis narratives major on human consciousness and the ambiguous moral situation in which people find themselves placed, in relation to one another, the natural world and religious faith. This points to a different kind of understanding of religion from that of an alternative kind of science.

Most people have experienced some form of ecstasy or, at least, a sense of something greater than themselves in which their self-awareness is taken up and changed. William Wordsworth describes this in 'Tintern Abbey' as the foundation of his poetic consciousness:

> For I have learned
> To look on nature, not as in the hour
> Of thoughtless youth, but hearing oftentimes
> The still, sad music of humanity,
> Nor harsh nor grating, though of ample power
> To chasten and subdue. And I have felt
> A presence that disturbs me with the joy
> Of elevated thoughts; a sense sublime
> Of something far more deeply interfused,
> Whose dwelling is the light of setting suns,
> And the round ocean, and the living air,
> And the blue sky, and in the mind of man,
> A motion and a spirit, that impels
> All thinking things, all objects of all thought,
> And rolls through all things.

For some, like Wordsworth, these moods or perceptions come in response to nature. For others it is a human relationship such as sexual love that lifts them out of themselves. Some would locate their self-transcendence in art, and some in the practices of religion.

For Christianity such experiences are not random or self-induced but indications that life has a sacred origin, dynamic and purpose. Life is not a possession or attribute of individuals themselves; individual existence beats within a wider pulse of being. At one level that is a straightforward biological reality: we are part of the web of life, natural and human. Yet we like to give priority to our separate awareness and desires, while actually being dependent on life patterns and forces far beyond our much prized individuality.

There are two contrasting ways of evaluating our undoubted dependence. Some argue that individual consciousness is an evolutionary by-product, useful in the wider scheme of development but not in itself an unqualified good or fulfilling purpose. Religion, in contrast, views consciousness as something that gives value not only to human life but to all existence because it is divine in origin. Neither our reason nor our experience can decide between these views, but it is not unreasonable to hold that human consciousness reflects something in the wider structure of reality.

That is what Christians are affirming when they say that 'God created the world'. But their belief is not primarily an intellectual theory about how things came to be. Rather Christians, like people of other faith traditions, are motivated to acknowledge something greater than themselves from which they derive energy and purpose. To encounter this wider reservoir of being is to shed the inhibitions and sharp-edged limitations of 'me', 'I' and 'you'. Then 'we' can breathe in a wider element through which a different kind of humanity might grow.

The idea of a divine Creator arises more from recognition and reverence than from an explanation of origins. Most religious traditions are extremely vague as to how God made the universe, falling far short of even rudimentary proto-scientific standards. The vital affirmation is that life is good because it is gifted to us and is something richer than human beings can invent or control. Religion is not sure exactly how life began or how it may end, but believes it has a divine origin and therefore a sacred purpose.

Creation stories have their own kind of metaphorical and moral truth. 'Let there be light' in Genesis is as much about 'seeing it was good' as it is about God switching on the cosmic light bulbs. When God walks in the garden in the cool of the day, we are not supposed to wonder whether he needed wellingtons. The divinity which 'made all things' is not to be conceived either as a superhuman colossus or a greybeard in the skies temporarily turned horticultural inspector. God is the mover and unfolding presence in all that happens.

The movement of creation is reverently and poetically depicted as deeply interfused in natural process. The Holy Spirit of God moves on the face of the waters as the breath of life. Light gives birth to a consciousness through which everything is conceived and in which human beings are empowered to describe, to relate, and to worship.

In time, humanity becomes self-conscious about this extraordinary yet troubling gift of consciousness, and makes distinctions that reveal not just good and evil, but the nature and purpose of divinity itself. That is because, as the Genesis narrative affirms, 'people are made in the image of God'. Human self-awareness echoes and arises from something in the universe around us. We are to a degree 'become like gods'.

Consciousness is part of biological function and is shared by humanity with many other life forms. But this consciousness of consciousness, the capacity to interact with our own self-awareness, and potentially to transcend and lose the normal self, seems so far to be a distinctively human attribute. In religion it is this capacity that connects us with the world and others, since it engages with the spiritual origin and sustaining of all life.

Reason forms an important part of humanity's expanded self-awareness, but our consciousness can never be wholly objective or detached. We are participant actors as well as potential playwrights. And religion welcomes rather than denies this truth.

To participate in religious terms is to worship by surrendering self to the mystery that animates consciousness. Reason is not thereby denied or devalued since it is a precious part of our self-awareness. But reason functions within a wider context, and everything we learn through reason has to be subject to further expansion and revision through our experience.

Without participation and self-surrender human consciousness becomes drab, habitual and constrained. Only by opening ourselves to what is other than self can we come to value and experience all forms of life. Knowledge needs to be two-way and relational if it is to truly enhance and enlighten. If consciousness is only a reflex of biological existence then we are imprisoned in ourselves and capable only of reacting rather than appreciating or enjoying; life loses its energy and radiance.

When we recognize and celebrate that which is beyond, beneath, above and around individual consciousness, then our awareness becomes multi-dimensional, enlivening and often unpredictable. By sharing with other beings we are able to change and grow. Consciousness becomes a source of beauty, love and delight rather than something to be feared, manipulated and controlled in subjection to the individual ego.

We are able to gather up a primal impulse to reverence each stream and flower, each tree, bird and rock, because they express divine creation; and, because our awareness of them is in itself an intimation of divine consciousness, a beat in the sacred rhythm. This insight runs like a golden thread through music and art and is superbly embodied in the Canticle or Praise Song which St Francis of Assisi conceived as he experienced the approach of death:

O Most High, most Potent, Sweet Lord,
To you belong the praise, the glory, the honour and all
    blessing.
To you alone, Most High, all look for life,
None can fitly speak Your Name.
With all your creatures, Lord, be praised,
Not least for Sir, our Brother Sun, who daily brings us light.

Beautiful and radiant in His great splendour,
How well he tells of Thee, Most High.
Be praised, my Lord, for Sister Moon and stars,
Carved by You, clear and rich and fair.
Be praised, my Lord, for Brother Wind,
For air in every mood and time through whom You give
Your creatures life.
Be praised, my Lord, for Sister Water,
So useful, humble, precious, pure.
Be praised, my Lord, for Brother Fire,
Which lightens us by night, fine, cheerful, strong.
Be praised, my Lord, for Mother Earth,
Who holds us up and keeps us straight, yields diverse fruits
and flowers of different colour.
O praise and bless my Lord
Thanking Him and serving Him with reverent honour.

Human consciousness does not come first in the Genesis account of creation's unfolding; it is a late emergence, as science both confirms and amplifies. From the start, long before humanity, the universe was a complex system nurturing life but also destroying it through violent conflict. When consciousness is born within that crucible it has to respond to what it can neither explain nor adequately control.

The origins of religion lie in doubt and perplexity rather than certainty. Religion has the capacity to evolve patterns of worship and practical living that respond to the problems as well as the joys of existence. When this capacity is hijacked to apply absolute claims or reinforce power structures that imitate secular models, then the primary characteristics of religion are weakened; its creative energies are diverted into non-religious purposes, and in the process distorted.

The codification of religion and the ethical implications of religious systems will be examined in the next chapter. But these systems are first and foremost a response to the questions of evil and wrongdoing. Religious faith holds that our consciousness is not an isolated by-product. Instead it connects with transformative moral, psychological, social and spiritual energies that may unify creation because of its divine purpose. This in turn can fulfil humanity's potential despite our flawed condition. In the words of the Hebrew psalmists, so often on Christ's lips, 'the earth is the Lord's', and as a result the 'kingdom of God' proclaimed by Jesus can bring human society and nature together.

However, Christianity cannot logically account for the origin – and sometimes prevalence – of wrongdoing or death-dealing violence. Nor does the Bible attempt to do so. The role and purpose of religion is to identify with a potential for life-affirming goodness which faith holds to be the divine origin and purpose of the universe. Religious insight enables people to discern and try to live in accord with a harmony that is incomplete and often broken.

Such an approach, based on faith, hope and love rather than on certainty, whether revealed or discovered, does not satisfy philosophers. Nor can it please those who want religion to be a substitute form of science. But it does accord with what we experience as human beings. At the centre of our existence is a mystery that we live through, yet cannot account for or ever fully resolve.

Julian of Norwich, a deeply practical medieval mystic, goes to the heart of the matter when she affirms that only in heaven can anyone understand why sin exists, wasting and destroying so much of creation. God, affirms Julian, does not blame people for their failings, seeking rather to restore their humanity to its full potential. Nor should people blame God as we do not understand the mystery. 'The cause of all this pain is sin,' Julian imagines the divine voice, 'but all shall be well, and all shall be well, and all manner of thing shall be well'.

In Christianity the counterpoint to evil and violence is redeeming sacrificial love. Few concepts in religion have been so open to abuse, and in Scotland the call for sacrifice has been used through the centuries to oppress as well as ennoble. Moreover, the need for self-sacrifice is often coupled with low self-esteem and a feeling of unworthiness.

Giving up individual desires and aspirations traditionally attracted social approval in Scotland, because such desires were held to be reprehensible or even shameful. The consequences of this surrender could be psychologically crippling, resulting in repression through external control, or in self-censorship diverting positive and natural energies into damagingly self-sacrificial channels. Iain Crichton Smith's novel *Consider the Lilies* is a classic exposition of these themes, looking at the consequences both for individuals and for Highland society as a whole of repressive nay-saying. Smith's study is based on the life of his own mother and carries an exceptional emotional charge.

Yet as Iain Crichton Smith's ironic title implies, this pervasive social psychology may have been based on a misunderstanding of Christianity, or at least of the teaching of Christ set out in the Christian Gospels. Why did Jesus die on a cross and what is the significance of that death for Christian patterns of living? Re-examining this crux is vital if Christianity is to find a new way of relating to Scottish society in the future. Without radical rethinking, Tom Nairn's oft quoted wish that the last minister be throttled with the last copy of the *Sunday Post* will surely come to be, because most people are no longer willing to be led to the altar of self-sacrifice like unthinking sheep, because the Church tells them to go.

In Christianity the cross, as both actuality and symbol, unites sin and sacrifice. The image is inescapable in Scottish art and architecture, as even the Calvinist iconoclasts held the cross before their inner eye. In all four Gospels the final conflict in Jerusalem forms the most extended and developed chapters, and some form of 'Passion Narrative' may have existed first, before the rest of the narrative, perhaps as a dramatic liturgy for Easter.

The New Testament Gospels paint the trial and execution of Jesus as the culmination of a cosmic conflict between good and evil. Many early Christians did literally believe that the formative events of their faith would trigger the end of the world. It seems pointless now to try to pin these apocalyptic sayings to actual events. What is essential and indisputable is that the Gospel writers accompany the human drama with a mood music of turbulence in spiritual realms. Some kind of new age is in its birth pangs.

Nevertheless, details of the arrest, trial and execution of Jesus are designed to be realistically vivid in psychological and social terms. We cannot now be sure of strict historical accuracy, but the main intent in any case lies elsewhere. The narratives draw repeated attention to the physical effects on Jesus' body and spirit of successive humiliations and violent assaults. This is because the whole drama is framed by 'sacred meals' expressing Jesus' own sacrifice through the sharing of food and drink: 'this is my body, this is my blood'. The willing passion and suffering of Jesus transforms his flesh and blood into an embodiment of God's love. As the New Testament writers have it, these are 'the first fruits' of the kingdom of God.

The cumulative power of this imagery, set within a superbly constructed drama, repays several readings of the Passion Narrative as a whole, rather than in the sections often prescribed. In literary terms it is unsurpassed, but what is its religious significance?

The death of Jesus on a wooden cross was a brutal and demeaning form of execution imposed by the Romans on 'barbarians', slaves and criminals. Christianity has understood it as a sacrificial death that, in some way, cancelled out the moral deficit of humanity. In the words of Mrs Cecil Alexander's Victorian hymn:

There was no other good enough
to pay the price of sin.
He only could unlock the door
of heaven and let us in.

This concept of 'paying the price' is more familiar than it is wholly clear. How can one person fairly or adequately take on himself the guilt and moral wrongdoing of millions? And besides, why would anyone in justice want them to do so?

The traditional answer is that the universe has an underlying moral order which was established by a just God. That moral law had to be satisfied and only Jesus could assume such a burden by 'taking on himself' the accumulated sins and wrong-doing of humanity past, present and future. In its full-blown version this theory of 'penal substitution' avers that justice requires punishment, so Jesus, 'God's own son', underwent this on our behalf.

Sometimes this idea is linked with the story of Abraham and Isaac in the Jewish Scriptures. The Hebrew patriarch is instructed to sacrifice his only son Isaac to God but, at the last moment, a young goat is provided by God as a substitute. So Isaac is spared, and Abraham's faith is justified. In traditional Christian exegesis the kid is seen as the antitype of Jesus 'the lamb of God'.

Linkage between these two narratives highlights the problem with the concept of a God who requires a price to be paid, a retribution for sin. It is deeply out of kilter with the loving Creator vividly evoked by Jesus in the Gospels. How can humanity place faith in a God whose love is conditioned by a primary demand for justice expressed as a punishment? Why should a loving Creator be bound to extract a price for human fallibility? Moreover, the idea that Jesus as a 'new Adam' can reverse the state of fallen-ness caused by the first Adam is tied up with the unconvincing notion that Adam's momentary foible could sink the human race in the moral mire for successive generations.

This traditional linkage between moral unworthiness, punishment and 'being obliged' to someone else for their sacrificial 'payment' had profoundly negative effects in Scotland. A culture of self-deprecation and obligation grew up, strengthened if not necessarily caused by this religious ethos. The causes may have been more to do with poverty and inequality than theology, but instead of challenging the social order, religious practice inculcated deference and discouraged individual initiative.

There is also a bias in such theological thinking towards the past; humanity is imprisoned by the consequences of history. Faith denies freedom. The teaching of the Christian Gospels by contrast is oriented towards the future; Jesus speaks constantly in the future tense. The kingdom of God is beginning to arrive, and will come, because Christ willingly undertakes his path of self-sacrifice in response to a loving Creator. It is a new creation that breaks the dominance of the past in favour of future possibility and potential.

In this sense Christ does 'pay the price of sin' in that he endures the worst humanity can perpetrate of violence, cruelty, injustice and degradation. But this is not required by God in the name of justice or punishment; the vital point is that these experiences are undergone by Jesus without any loss of love and compassion for all humanity. Everything is suffered and forgiven because love is the will and intention of the Creator with whom Christ totally identifies, and with whom he desires to be entirely reunited. According to Duns Scotus, the Scottish Franciscan philosopher, Christ's incarnation as a human being was always part of creation's unfolding and not a result of 'the fall'. As Luke portrays it in his Gospel, even the common criminal hanging on a cross beside Jesus is caught up in the movement of redemptive love – 'today you will be with me in Paradise'.

The critical point here is that what is given is beyond price. Only something uncalculated and exceptional can reverse the deficit of moral cause and effect. There is no equalizing of the scales, but an outpouring of generosity that is beyond calculation or measure of any kind. This kind of irrational giving is what has enabled self-conscious creation in the first place, and gives it purpose. What is then further given by Christ, in the same spirit of divine love, is free and without limit – grace abounding and amazing. The mystery of love moves us through and beyond the enigma of evil.

This quality of unrestricted, all-encompassing love reveals Christ in the New Testament as distinctively 'of God'. His free sacrifice is an inclusive and potentially representative act, because it has the power to freely attract human response and participation. The divine spirit in Jesus creates a new and closer union with God, so releasing a loving energy with the capacity to realize the original purpose of creation in ways we cannot yet imagine. It is the future that counts. God is with humanity in a more intimate relationship that is messier and yet richer and deeper than any idealized state of immortal perfection. This new 'kingdom of God' commences with Jesus, but human beings – such as the struggling disciples – are only beginning to discover what it may mean.

Yet there is still a major obstacle, a last enemy, which is death. Death is humanity's final hurdle, the undoing of love. If life can be ended by hate, violence and oppression, then the self-sacrifice of Jesus appears an idealistic but futile action. But the Gospel writers are already committed to a love who can overcome illness as well as evil, and even reverse death. So what have they to say about Jesus' own death which all four Gospels record as a definite historical event?

There is no shirking the universal experience that death is decisive and overwhelming for our common humanity. Death requires rites of mourning, burial and remembrance. The physical body is broken but then tenderly taken, bathed, anointed, wrapped in a shroud, and laid in a dark tomb in the earth. Then what?

Early on the first day of the week, while it was still dark, Mary Magdalene went to the tomb and saw that the stone had been removed from the entrance. So she came running to Simon Peter and the other disciple, the one Jesus loved, and said, 'They have taken the Lord out of the tomb, and we don't know where they have put him!'

So Peter and the other disciple started for the tomb. Both were running, but the other disciple outran Peter and reached the tomb first. He bent over and looked in at the strips of linen lying there but did not go in. Then Simon Peter, who was behind him, arrived and went into the tomb. He saw the strips of linen lying there, as well as the burial cloth that had been around Jesus' head. The cloth was folded up by itself, separate from the linen. Finally the other disciple, who had reached the tomb first, also went inside. He saw and believed. (They still did not understand from Scripture that Jesus had to rise from the dead.)

Then the disciples went back to their homes, but Mary stood outside the tomb crying. As she wept, she bent over to look into the tomb and saw two angels in white, seated where Jesus' body had been, one at the head and the other at the foot.

They asked her, 'Woman, why are you crying?'

'They have taken my Lord away,' she said, 'and I don't know where they have put him.' At this, she turned round and saw Jesus standing there, but she did not realise that it was Jesus.

'Woman,' he said, 'why are you crying? Who is it you are looking for?'

Thinking he was the gardener, she said, 'Sir, if you have carried him away, tell me where you have put him, and I will get him.'

Jesus said to her, 'Mary.'

She turned towards him and cried out in Aramaic, 'Rabboni!' (which means Teacher).

Jesus said, 'Do not hold on to me, for I have not yet returned to the Father. Go instead to my brothers and tell them, 'I am returning to my Father and your Father, to my God and your God.'

Mary Magdalene went to the disciples with the news: 'I have seen the Lord!' And she told them that he had said these things to her.

John 20.1–18

The resurrection evoked in the Gospels is the end of Jesus' life story, as biographically understood, and the beginning of Christianity. But the new faith remains rooted in a personal encounter or relationship that has survived death, changed but not diminished – Jesus said to her 'Mary'.

The Gospels ask us to re-examine the experience of death in the light of love, as exemplified by Christ's self-sacrifice.

Like birth, they suggest, death is a mystery: the transition to a different way of being. On a scientific level death is a metamorphosis from one organic unity to a new set of biological elements. Culturally, too, death is not a final end since the dead live in our dreams, memories and emotions. But what the Gospels describe is a persistence of consciousness, a continuing unity of body, mind and spirit in a way that sustains people's identity and their capacity to love and be loved as distinct individuals. It is this experience of 'death in love' and divine love in death that renders biological cessation the passage to a stronger, deeper sense of life. Jesus, teacher of God's kingdom, has opened the way to a kind of life that can outlast even death.

Christian faith is conceived in this mysterious New Testament experience. But how is it to be understood or sustained by those outside the first community of Christ's friends and disciples? This brings us back full circle to the purpose and patterns of religion in society.

# 8

# Freedom and Love

'Religion' is based on the Latin word *religio* which comes from a root meaning to tie, connect or bind. The 'good life' in religious terms is that which connects or binds humanity together through shared purpose and to mutual benefit. Religion is therefore lived out or expressed socially as well as personally. It is about relationships that make for community among people, and between people and the wider web of life. Even solitariness in religion is a mode of connecting.

A defining test for religion is therefore how it relates to its social environments. Is any given religious tradition a sect, isolated from its context, or is it engaged with the wider community? In practice, religions define themselves according to whether their field of interest is society as a whole, or only those who subscribe to a set of specific beliefs and practices which form in turn an enclosed social subset.

Another factor is the nature of communication between the religious community and society as a whole. One option is a concordat that recognizes distinctive roles and encourages mutual influences. Another option is conflict or suppression in one direction or the other. Religion may express its beliefs as a kind of command that obliges obedience, or encourage a dialogue between faith's expressions and other perspectives. Typically there are many gradations in between.

These relationships are influenced by different political systems, and by the degree of diversity tolerated within society. But they are also shaped by the kind of belief system at work. Theology may emphasize a bridge between the faith community and a divinely created world, or stress the gap between the holy group and a faithless, sinful world.

What, then, in real terms, is a good life and how can we practise it? In Jewish understanding, the people of God are called to live out the Torah which is the divine way or law revealed on Mount Sinai. For Moslems, the path to a good life lies through collective obedience to the teaching of the Koran, and the observance of associated Islamic custom and law.

Hinduism teaches a way of religious obedience that ties the individual stages of life with social structures and spiritual experience. In Buddhism, which places great emphasis on individual discipline, there is also a collective community of faith, the Sangha, which gives religious and social context to each person's quest for enlightenment. In Christianity, the faithful are called to be citizens of the kingdom of God rather than solitary believers.

All of these religions now operate in Scotland, but this account will focus on Christianity because it provides a comparison between past and present that will also throw light on other faiths.

The life and teaching of Jesus of Nazareth, as embodied in the New Testament Gospels, is defining for Christian understanding. As a Jew, Jesus draws extensively on the idea of an organized community that is faithful to the God who created all things and who desires humanity to flourish in peace, justice and creativity. Such a community can be summed up in the Hebrew word *shalom*, which is not the absence of conflict but an active, fruitful and dynamic harmony that includes all, not least the marginalized and the outsider.

Like earlier Hebrew prophets, Christ measures society in all its aspects against these values and finds it wanting. Even (perhaps especially) the representatives of organized religion – whose job it is to announce, encourage and sustain *shalom* – seem busy reinforcing their own interests rather than the common good:

'Woe to you, Pharisees, because you give to God a tenth of your mint, rue and all other kinds of garden herbs, but you

94

neglect justice and the love of God; you should have practised the latter without leaving the former undone.

Woe to you, Pharisees, because you love the most important seats in the synagogues, and greetings in the market-places.

Woe to you, because you are like unmarked graves, which people walk over without knowing it.'

One of the experts in the law answered him, 'Teacher, when you say these things you insult us also.'

Jesus replied, 'And, you experts in the law, woe to you, because you load people down with burdens they can hardly carry, and you yourselves will not lift one finger to help them.'

'Woe to you, because you build tombs for the prophets, and it was your ancestors who killed them. So you testify that you approve of what your ancestors did: they killed the prophets, and you build their tombs.'

Luke 11.42–48

This may not be a comprehensive picture of the religious authorities in Jesus' time, but that would be to miss the point. There is an underlying tendency in all societies for organized religion to be diverted from community building to church, synagogue or temple building. Christ exposes that with penetrating verve.

Jesus' style of thought and expression is poetic. He uses images, metaphors and stories to provoke understanding, and some of the language is paradoxical and playful. His teachings are like seeds planted in the mind, heart and imagination so that, in due time, they will bear fruit in illumination and action. There is no attempt to systematize or categorize the 'way of the kingdom', no book of rules. To discover what it is all about, listeners have to start on a journey.

Much the same could be said of Christ's actions. They too are parables or dramas that express the kingdom of God. Some commentators have emphasized the shaping of the four Gospel narratives by early Christian communities after Jesus' death.

The communities are both authors and editors. But it is also clear that Jesus himself was fully aware of the wider significance of his actions, which are deeply rooted in his own consciousness of God.

An interesting example of this is the baptism of Jesus by John the Baptiser at the beginning of John's Gospel. As Jesus rises from the River Jordan the Holy Spirit of God hovers over the scene just as the Spirit or breath of God 'moved on the face of the waters' at the moment of creation in the Book of Genesis. The symbolic words 'This is my beloved Son' are then heard.

This account is imbued with Jewish Scriptures and the early Christian belief that initiation into Christianity is 'becoming a child of God' through Jesus. But behind all of these connections is Jesus' own visionary experience. The awareness of God encapsulated in the baptism is borne out in Jesus' words and actions throughout the Gospels. It is, therefore, likely that on one level the narrative reaches back into Jesus' own consciousness and his memory of this formative event as shared with his intimate friends and followers.

Recent research, supported by the discovery of many primary source texts at Qumran by the Red Sea, suggests that Jesus may have been part of a radical, mystical and potentially revolutionary movement to recover the religion of the First Temple, which existed before the Jewish elite were exiled to Babylon. The main emphasis was not on obedience to a legal scripture or code, which was to become the hallmark of Rabbinic Judaism, but on a divine union with the God who made the universe.

That link is consistent with the connection made throughout the Gospels between seeking the kingdom of God and following Jesus – becoming his companions on the way. It is not a matter of accepting a new religious law or a new philosophy or even a new set of beliefs. This is about beginning a new way of living in relationship with the divine sources of life itself. The message is clear in Jesus' own teaching and is then reflected in the structure of the Gospels which offer Jesus' life and death as a pattern to be lived out. By following Jesus, companions become disciples and Christians. It is primarily a matter of participating and experiencing rather than a creed or moral code.

From the start, Christ's moral and spiritual teaching takes an unconventional direction. Popular belief then, and perhaps now, associated divine favour with prosperity and good fortune. But Jesus' line is that misfortune, poverty, loss and powerlessness are more likely to be signs of blessing.

> Blessed are the poor in spirit, for theirs is the kingdom of heaven.
> Blessed are those who mourn, for they will be comforted.
> Blessed are the meek, for they will inherit the earth.
> Blessed are those who hunger and thirst for righteousness, for they will be filled.

> Matthew 5.3–6

Jesus continues his blessings or 'beatitudes' with qualities that would be reasonably familiar to his Jewish listeners:

> Blessed are the merciful, for they will be shown mercy.
> Blessed are the pure in heart, for they will see God.
> Blessed are the peacemakers, for they will be called children of God.
> Blessed are those who are persecuted because of righteousness, for theirs is the kingdom of heaven.

> Matthew 5.7–10

None the less, most would expect God's blessing to be demonstrated in some material way. Virtue should be rewarded.

Is Jesus' teaching, then, an Orthodox restatement of the Jewish Torah or a radical departure? Typically this disconcerting new voice takes the paradoxical route of claiming that it is both:

Do not think that I have come to abolish the law, or the prophets: I have not come to abolish them, but to fulfil them.

For verily I say unto you, until heaven and earth disappear, not the smallest letter, not the least stroke of a pen, will by any means disappear from the law until everything is accomplished.

Anyone who breaks one of the least of these commandments and teaches others to do the same will be called least in the kingdom of heaven; but whoever practises and teaches these commands, will be called great in the kingdom of heaven.

For I tell you that unless your righteousness surpasses that of the Pharisees and the teachers of the law, you will certainly not enter the kingdom of heaven.

Matthew 5.17–20

The challenge here is not just to conventional religious interpretation and practice. Obedience to conventional morality or religious custom is not enough. Instead Jesus urges a radical path of goodness, an active calling that transcends traditional labelling:

You are the salt of the earth: but if the salt loses its saltiness, how can it be made salty again? It is no longer good for anything. Except to be thrown out, and trampled underfoot.

You are the light of the world. A city on a hill cannot be hidden.

Neither do people light a lamp, and put it under a bowl, instead they put it on its stand; and it gives light to everyone in the house.

In the same way, let your light shine before others, that they may see your good deeds, and praise your Father in heaven.

Matthew 5.13–16

What does this mean in terms of life lived? Is it just a playing with language, a metaphorical game, pointing to some elusive mystical experience? There is a spiritual invitation involved, but the follow-through is also uncomfortably clear.

The moral law says that murder is wrong; what Christ teaches is a 'conversion of the heart' that uproots anger and hate. The moral law condemns adultery, but Jesus targets lust. The moral law prescribes legal adjudication, but Christ advocates peace-making ahead of court judgements. The moral law approves a proportionate response to violence, but Jesus preaches non-violence:

> You have heard that it was said, 'Eye for eye, and tooth for tooth.'
>
> But I tell you, Do not resist an evil person. If someone strikes you on the right cheek, turn the other cheek also.
>
> And if someone wants to sue you, and take your tunic, hand over your cloak as well.
>
> If someone forces you to go one mile, go two miles.
>
> Give to the one who asks you, and do not turn away from the one who wants to borrow from you.
>
> Matthew 5.38–42

The moral law says 'love your neighbour', but Christ's version is 'love your enemies and do good to those who hate you'. You cannot circumscribe who qualifies as a 'neighbour'. The moral law advocates diligent religious observance so that goodness can be socially reinforced. For Jesus, the practice of religion should be centred on God 'who sees what is done according to the heart in secret'. External moral judgements are worthless; people should learn to see as God sees:

> Do not judge, or you too will be judged.
>
> For in the same way as you judge others, you will be judged; and with the measure you use, it will be measured to you.
>
> And why do you look at the speck of sawdust in someone else's eye and pay no attention to the plank in your own eye?

How can you say, 'Let me take the speck out of your eye' when all the time there is a plank in your own eye?

You hypocrite, first take the plank out of your own eye; and then you will see clearly to remove the speck from the other person's eye.

Matthew 7.1–5

At the core of this vision is faith in a divine Creator who cares for each part of creation with intimate knowledge and love. That granted, normal expectations or assessments of success and security are turned on their head:

Therefore I tell you, do not worry about your life, what you will eat, or drink; or about your body, what you will wear. Is not life more important than food, and the body than clothes?

Look at the birds of the air: they do not sow or reap or store away in barns and yet your heavenly Father feeds them. Are you not much more valuable than they?

Who of you by worrying can add a single hour to your life?

And why do you worry about clothes? See how the lilies of the field grow. They do not labour or spin.

Yet I tell you that not even Solomon in all his splendour was dressed like one of these.

If that is how God clothes the grass of the field, which is here today and tomorrow is thrown into the fire, will he not much more clothe you, O you of little faith?

So do not worry, saying, 'What shall we eat?' or 'What shall we drink'? or 'What shall we wear?'

For the pagans run after all these things, and your heavenly Father knows that you need them.

But seek first his kingdom and his righteousness, and all these things will be to you as well.

Therefore do not worry about tomorrow: for tomorrow will worry about itself. Each day has enough trouble of its own.

Matthew 6.25–34

This is one of the most eloquent passages in any of the world's sacred texts, yet also one of the most fundamentally incredible from the standpoint of normal human experience. How could people follow this teaching?

The keys to the kingdom of God are, for Christ, wholehearted trust in a loving Creator or heavenly Father who sets aside normal expectations. The harsh lessons of human experience, the legacy of past suffering and wrongs, are forgiven. Only an ability to reverse distrust, resentment and fear can foster good relations between all parts of creation – *shalom*. Through forgiveness the purpose of creation can be recovered:

> For if you forgive others when they sin against you, your heavenly Father will also forgive you:
> But if you do not forgive others their sins, your Father will not forgive your sins.
>
> Matthew 6.14–15

The same purpose of making good what is out of joint animates the prayer of God's kingdom which Jesus taught his followers to say:

> He said to them, 'When you pray, say, "Our Father, Hallowed be your name. Your kingdom come. Your will be done, as in heaven, so in earth.
> Give us each day our daily bread.
> And forgive us our sins; for we also forgive everyone who sins against us.
> And lead us not into temptation; but deliver us from evil"'.
>
> Luke 11.2–4

None of this can be absorbed by rote or rule, since all depends on seeing things in a new light. The whole thrust is counter-intuitive, until and unless humanity can see as God sees, realigning with the purpose of creation:

Ask, and it will be given to you; seek, and you will find; knock, and the door will be opened to you:

For everyone who asks receives; everyone who seeks finds; and to everyone who knocks the door will be opened.

Which of you, if your children ask for bread, will give them a stone?

Or if they ask for a fish, will give them a snake?

If you then, though you are evil, know how to give good gifts to your children, how much more will your Father in heaven give good gifts to those who ask him!

Matthew 7.7–11

It is clear within the Gospels that not everyone is likely to accept or try out this paradoxical teaching. Though those who do so will be wise, like those who build their house on rock rather than sand, they may constitute a small minority:

Enter through the narrow gate. For wide is the gate, and broad is the road that leads to destruction, and many enter through it.

But small is the gate and narrow the road that leads to life and only a few find it.

Matthew 7.13–14

Even more perplexing to Jesus' audiences then and now is the reiteration that religious belief and practice do not in themselves open the way to the kingdom of God:

Not everyone who says to me, 'Lord, Lord', will enter the kingdom of heaven; but only those who do the will of my Father who is in heaven.

Many will say to me on that day, 'Lord, Lord, did we not prophesy in your name? And in your name drive out demons and perform many miracles?'

And then I will tell them plainly, 'I never knew you. Away from me, you evildoers.'

Matthew 7: 21–23

This imagery of entry and inclusion is taken up and developed in John's Gospel which pictures Jesus and his teaching as 'The Gate of the Sheepfold' and as 'The Way, the Truth and the Life'.

The New Testament Gospels present a honed compendium of Jesus' teaching, much of which was originally passed on through oral memory and repetition. They represent in a compressed form many different occasions and versions of a message that seems vivid, attractive, challenging, poetic, puzzling and elusive. The kingdom of God embodies the good way of life, but how does it play out in actual lives?

Christ teaches, enacts, tells stories and dramatizes in a unified appeal to mind, heart and imagination. It is in this context that the 'healing miracles' of Jesus are to be understood since these encounters are about much more than physical health. To enter the kingdom of God is to recover health or wholeness as the purpose of creation and an integral part of *shalom*. Illness is similar to moral wrongdoing or injustice in that it disrupts the well-being that God desires and intends for all living things. That makes Jesus a healer of physical, mental and spiritual wounds.

Like Job in the Jewish Scriptures, Jesus rejects the idea that sickness is a sign of God's disfavour or necessarily linked to human wrongdoing. The Gospels depict Jesus releasing healing energies that are divine in origin. This is part of the same active love that can forgive sins and restore relationships, as well as transcend disabilities, transform mental illness and, in the psychiatry of the day, 'cast out demons'.

But such 'cures' are not external magic. They depend on the openness of those concerned to healing or, as Jesus expresses it, to the restorative holistic power of the Creator, as this extended passage shows:

While he was saying this, a ruler came and knelt before him, saying, 'My daughter has just died. But come and put your hand on her, and she will live'. Jesus got up, and went with him, and so did his disciples.

Just then a woman, who had been subject to bleeding for twelve years, came up to him, and touched the edge of his cloak. She said to herself, 'If I only touch his cloak, I will be healed.'

Jesus turned and saw her. 'Take heart, daughter' he said, 'your faith has healed you.' And the woman was healed from that moment.

When Jesus entered the ruler's house and saw the flute players and the noisy crowd, he said, 'Go away. The girl is not dead, but asleep.' But they laughed at him. After the crowd had been put outside, he went in and took the girl by the hand, and she got up. News of this spread through all that region.

As Jesus went on from there two blind men followed him, calling out, 'Have mercy on us, Son of David!'

And when he had gone indoors, the blind men came to him: and he asked them, 'Do you believe that I am able to do this?' 'Yes, Lord', they replied.

Then he touched their eyes and said, 'According to your faith will it be done to you.' And their sight was restored; Jesus warned them sternly, 'See that no-one knows about this.' But they went out and spread the news about him all over that region.

While they were going out, a man who was demon-possessed and could not talk was brought to Jesus. And when the demon was driven out, the man who had been mute spoke. The crowd was amazed and said, 'Nothing like this has ever been seen in Israel.'

But the Pharisees said, 'It is by the prince of demons that he drives out demons.'

Matthew 9.18–34

These narratives of healing also have a subtext: Jesus tries to avoid publicity because he does not wish his religious teaching to be obscured by the all-too-human obsession with wonder-working. He does not intend to cancel out medical wisdom but to complete it. Jesus does not court media sensation but inward conversion. This is well illustrated by two encounters that are expanded in John's Gospel as dialogues.

First Jesus meets a Samaritan woman at the well and asks her to draw him a drink of water. Strict Jews in Jesus' time regarded the Samaritans as not only inferior but ritually unclean, making their drinking vessels 'untouchable'. This request is the starting point for a discussion on water which will become 'a spring welling up to eternal life'. So the everyday yet elemental act of sharing water leads to a challenge to prejudice, an exploration of faith, and then a moral re-evaluation of personal life on the woman's part. Jesus too is touched and moved. A healing process has begun in a simple action of tenderness and boundary crossing. No physical cure is involved.

That incident can be set alongside Jesus' meeting with the man who sits by the Pool of Bethsaida, hoping to enter the water first after it is stirred or moved so as to be cured of his paralysis. But he has no one to help him into the Pool. When Jesus perceives the man's desire to be whole and his conviction he will be cured, however misplaced, he instructs him to 'pick up your mat and walk'. In this case the physical healing completes a psychological readiness and spiritual determination. It is important in these narratives to recognize that Jesus' miracles are a direct expression of God's active loving will to remake creation, rather than a demonstration of folk medicine or faith healing.

These encounters then, as a whole, demonstrate that God is a loving Creator concerned for each individual in his or her own right, regardless of race, social status, genetic condition or religious creed. They also enact the teaching or wise sayings of Jesus.

A third complementary layer of exposition lies in the stories told by Jesus in the Gospels, particularly the three parables of love.

First, there is the story of the lost sheep. God, implies Jesus, is like a shepherd who, even though he has 99 sheep safely folded, heads out and devotes all his efforts to retrieving the one lost sheep. And the shepherd brings this missing individual safely home with greater joy and satisfaction than he has derived from the secure majority.

This flies in the face of every statistical measure or rational policy. But it is in accord with the kingdom of God since each living being is distinctively and individually loved rather than representatively or collectively valued. Love in the abstract does not count with God.

A second parable involves the definition of neighbourliness to which reference has already been made. In this story a traveller is attacked by robbers and left on the roadside to die. Two pillars of religious society pass by averting their gaze, but an outcast, despised Samaritan stops, tends the man's wounds, and takes him to an inn to recover at his rescuer's own expense. Now, says Jesus, who was a true neighbour to this victim of violent crime? Those in his own social and religious structure or the 'unclean' stranger?

A third story of love comes closer to the familial core. It concerns a father and his two sons. The younger impatiently claims his share of the family wealth and heads off to 'a far country'. The father could have refused this claim, but gives his son liberty of choice. Gradually the young man loses all he has and becomes a swine-herd 'who longed to fill his stomach with the pods that the pigs were eating'. Eventually he decides to head home and ask his father's forgiveness.

The father sees his lost son approaching and, instead of standing on his patriarchal dignity, rushes like a loving mother to hug and welcome the boy home. Then he orders a party to celebrate. The elder brother, who has remained dutiful and hardworking throughout, bitterly resents this lavish greeting. But the father simultaneously affirms and rebukes his older son, 'You are always with me and everything I have is yours. But we have to celebrate and be glad because this brother of yours was dead and is alive again; he was lost and is found.'

The narrative of the prodigal son, or perhaps the prodigal father, has the touch of genius. That is because it takes the most powerful and intimate of human emotions, parental love, and shows how that instinct brings us close to God our heavenly father. God's love comes to humankind as an abundant, free, unearned grace, not as an obligation or reward.

Christ has much to say, enact and story about the good life and how it may be understood in the light of God's kingdom. But most of it upends conventional understandings of the role of the Christian Church, and of the nature of morality. Instead of being lauded as the conduit of religious truth, organized religion is excoriated as a blocked channel. Easy assumptions about social morality are swept aside as hypocritical.

The major Churches have blamed their decline on a lack of religious feeling in the wider society, but in early twenty-first-century Scotland people are turning away from institutional Christianity because of its failure of religious vision. This prophetic critique leaves the link between organized religion and conventional morality in twentieth-century Scotland badly exposed. It would be hard to move honestly from the life and teaching of Christ to the kind of institutional compromises and complacency that have characterized institutional religion in recent Scottish history.

Of course Christ's teaching anticipates and receives a hostile reaction. Were living a good life natural or easy, then there would be no need for religion, far less Christianity. The New Testament Gospels evoke a reality that involves conflict and struggle. From the start Jesus is up against the religious authorities of the day. But it gets worse as he transgresses the taboos of race, class and gender as well as religion. Moreover, Christ's critique of materialism strikes at the mercantile basis of an unequal society then and now.

This morally driven challenge to convention and prejudice stirs conflict in communities and in families, as evidenced in the Gospels by the troubled reactions of Christ's own family. Moreover, in the Palestine of Jesus such challenge is also politically charged, for the 'province' of Judea is not an independent nation but part of the Roman Empire. This sets the scene for a drama of accumulating tension between religious, social, political and imperial perspectives.

It is all terrifyingly familiar to twenty-first-century eyes. The Jewish authorities, with whom Jesus initially clashes, treat any threat to their jurisdiction as a potential trigger for reprisals on the part of the occupying imperial power. Popular nationalist protest is ever at the ready while many Judeans, including the hated tax gatherers, have a vested interest in the unequal status quo. The mix is, to say the least, combustible.

Yet the Gospel narratives, like a Greek tragedy, are not limited to humanistic drama. They view these earthbound conflicts within a wider cosmic struggle between good and evil. In fact, the social and political disputes, as well as divisions within organized religion, are implied rather than expounded. What is foregrounded by the Gospel writers is a conflict in spiritual realms, as the creation of a good and loving God is riven by hate, violence and prejudice.

Where does this leave twenty-first-century Christianity in Scotland? While conflict between the vision of God's kingdom and the reality is to be expected, the disjunction between the New Testament and where Scotland's major Churches have ended up is disturbing. Moreover, the safety-first approach of the Churches has been wholly counterproductive. On the present trajectory the main Christian institutions will be a barely recognizable rump within a generation. Could there be an alternative future, for religion and for Scotland? And how could Christianity as conceived in the New Testament contribute to such a scenario?

# 9

# Faith in the Future

The discernible future of Christianity in Scotland will be as a minority faith, within which there will continue to be diverse interpretations of core principles. Other world religions will also play an integral part in Scotland's multifaith society.

Despite the hopes of some secular humanists it is unlikely that religious faith and practice will disappear. The sensibilities, imagination and psychological needs that nurture religion are deeply layered. Only a few totalitarian regimes have succeeded in suppressing organized religion, providing instead state and leader worship, but religious faith has returned to haunt – and in some cases help to topple – them. A uniformly secular Scotland is an improbable but also a dull prospect.

Equally any oppressive religious order is undesirable and, as Scotland demonstrates, damaging in the long run to the vitality and effectiveness of religious faith itself. The alternative scenario of minority religion can of course go in different directions, as previously described. A faith tradition may become a defensive subculture minimizing its relationship with the wider society in the name of purity, or it may strive to actively engage with and influence its environment.

This brief study shows that the sources of Christianity lie in outward-looking engagement. The seeds of Christ's 'kingdom of God' have to be scattered widely to take effect, even if many of these endeavours appear to have no immediate impact. The New Testament Gospels presume that only a minority of people will become active followers and that even they will struggle to understand their vocation. None the less, the vision articulated is universal in its scope, embracing humanity, divinity and nature.

The Christian Gospels are not focused on establishing an organized religion, but with practising a moral and spiritual anthropology that illumines all life, regardless of race, creed, gender, culture or class. This is the fertile power of Christianity that most Churches have devoted much energy and ingenuity to confining. There are no institutional or intellectual barriers set by Christ, only the invitation to begin on a compelling journey.

Christ's open door invitation to follow and learn runs counter to the general perception that a definite belief or set of beliefs is necessary to cross the Christian threshold. This misperception has often been reinforced by Churches for institutional reasons, by attaching certain credal formulas and commitments to admission or initiation. It is also reinforced by the sterile God debate between atheists and fundamentalists who trade blows over an abstract entity that bears small relation to any religious practice.

The invitation to journey involves ideas, values, emotions and imaginings interwoven around and through whole life experience. Many people may explore Christian perspectives, though choose not to embrace them for a time if at all. Many may only discover the validity of some aspect of Christian faith through a practical experience unconnected with organized religion. Some have found a pathway into Christian understanding through other faith traditions without abandoning their own background. Many, perhaps a majority, may profess faith in hope and love rather than individual conviction, depending on the faith community to which they belong to carry their understanding collectively. Some may vigorously profess their convictions in a way that lacks lived-out understanding.

In the Gospel pattern, all of these perspectives have a place in the community of faith. The images of journey, shared table and healing, are open-ended and inclusive. People may be in different places at different stages, but all are welcome. Disciples are those who learn together how far and how fully they can realize the Christian mysteries in their own lives. No part of this argument denies the importance of reflective ideas in shaping Christian understanding and communication. Reason is a valued gift, but so are imagination and empathy. Reflection can guide and inspire but remains secondary to the lived experience. Discovery comes before reflection.

If this approach is correct, then there are consequences for how Christian faith communities need to organize themselves. The emphasis should always be on openness and accessibility. Faith grows through a dialogue with other perspectives and insights, so collaboration with other faiths and with civil society becomes integral, rather than something that is added on to the core activities. This is essential for the learning journey, but also for ensuring that Christianity can contribute without distortion or prejudice. Christ uses metaphors of seeds, light, yeast and salt to show how his way of faith influences by participation, not by distance or alienation.

The future of Christianity as a creative, engaged minority within Scottish society requires rethinking the Church–society relationship in a more open way. This involves revising how faith communities operate to avoid the trap of clubs for the religiously inclined. But it also means changing defensive habits of mind which have over the centuries become a default reflex. One of these is the presumption that faith communities are the repositories of a religious truth that endows them with special authority. Truth in Christianity is the living out of Christ's way in faith, hope and love. This way does not confer authority or power, a claim that reflects the kind of worldly thinking that the Gospels explicitly undermine. Authenticity of experience and action, rather than authority, is the measure of Christianity.

Claims to religious authority in Christian tradition are usually based either on particular offices or roles that are held to be divinely appointed or on the Bible as a divine revelation, or a combination of the two. The first includes the arguments for papal authority in Roman Catholicism and for the role of bishops in general, which are in turn based on the authority of the Bible supplemented by early church history.

These arguments fall into the trap of biblical literalism to which attention has already been drawn. Though letters written to early Christian communities, which are preserved in the New Testament, refer to people called bishops and other roles, the picture is very fluid and indefinite. The main emphasis is on the organic nature of the faith community with different roles being assigned according to gifts and needs. There is no constitutional manual for church government in the Bible. A divine commission is given to all the disciples to fulfil Christ's purpose, not to any particular office or position. Of course some leadership roles were established early, and carry a weight of tradition. But it is the usefulness of such roles in serving the wider purpose of the community that counts, not any innate authority.

This subsidiary issue of church governance, which has caused so much conflict, also raises the larger issue of the Bible as a divine revelation. Most Christians agree that the writings of the Old and New Testaments are authoritative and defining for Christianity, but what do they actually mean? The Roman Catholic solution to diversity or conflict was to give papal authority the last word on scriptural interpretation. The Protestant Reformers reversed this on the grounds that the papacy had become self-serving and unchristian. But they disagreed among themselves on key points of doctrine, while holding that the 'Holy Spirit' would guide them to the 'self-evident' truths of the Bible. While both approaches have been historically influential, both have at points in history brought Christianity into disrepute, and the validity of the Bible as a source of moral or spiritual authority is now brought into question as never before.

Understanding the significance of the biblical texts is bound up with trying to authentically live out their values and purposes. This requires something from both the Catholic and the Protestant perspectives. The sacred Scriptures are foundational to the faith community as a guide and inspiration, but the community itself has to be their interpreter. This involves worship, reflection and practical experiment. Only a live interaction between Bible and faith community can nurture discipleship.

The inherited experience of Churches comes into play along with contemporary innovation.

Questions of faith and authentic interpretation are inevitably bound up with the nature of Churches as Christian communities. There is no one comprehensive, authoritative definition of Christianity, but a diversity of approaches that can complement one another and help build up a fuller picture, and richer outworkings of faith. All are by definition experimental, contributing to the realization of something that is in the future rather than the past. The New Testament itself tells a story of diversity and unity as Christianity spread to different regions, and encountered a variety of cultures, religions and political situations, first within the confines of the Roman Empire but then beyond its borders. Is there anything from this formative period that can help Christianity renew its relationship with twenty-first-century Scotland?

There are three creation stories in the Christian Bible. The first comes at the beginning of the Book of Genesis and evokes the sacred origin of the universe from the perspective of human consciousness and reverence. The second comes in the Gospels at the start of the New Testament and relates a new birth of humanity in Jesus Christ, through the medium of Mary, Mother of God. The third creation story concerns the birth of the Church at Pentecost, inspired by the same Holy Spirit that stirred the face of the waters in Genesis, and 'came upon' Mary in a willingly received divine conception. The Pentecost story is accorded much less attention than the other two, yet it has an equal importance in the unfolding of Christianity as a religious faith:

> When the day of Pentecost came, they were all together in one place. Suddenly a sound like the blowing of a violent wind came from heaven and filled the whole house where they were sitting. They saw what seemed to be tongues of fire that separated and came to rest on each one of them. All of them were filled with the Holy Spirit and began to speak in other languages as the Spirit enabled them.

Now there were staying in Jerusalem God-fearing Jews from every nation under heaven. When they heard this sound, a crowd came together in bewilderment, because each one heard them speaking in his or her own language. Utterly amazed, they asked: 'Are not all these who are speaking Galileans? Then how is it that each of us hears them in our own native language? Parthians, Medes and Elamites; residents of Mesopotamia, Judea and Cappadocia, Pontus and Asia, Phrygia and Pamphylia, Egypt and the parts of Libya near Cyrene; visitors from Rome (both Jews and converts to Judaism); Cretans and Arabs – we hear them declaring the wonders of God in our own tongues!' Amazed and perplexed, they asked one another, 'What does this mean?'

Acts 2.1–12

Many commentators since have also been perplexed about the meaning of this account. A whole school of Pentecostal interpretation has grown up based on a form of Spirit possession or inspiration, that enables Christian disciples then and since to speak in a special kind of language beyond words. But the story is very specific that each nationality and culture represented heard the disciples' utterances in their own language, not an alternative form of speech. The narrator also takes immense care to list all the various regions represented, as if to demonstrate the diversity that had to be overcome and expressed.

The Pentecost story can be read as reversing the Genesis account of the Tower of Babel, which thwarts a human desire for universal communication in favour of the 'babble' of competing tongues. But Pentecost transcends rather than reverses Babel, since the shared inspiration of the Holy Spirit embraces the diversity of human language and culture. The implication could not be clearer: Christianity affirms and brings together the diversity of humanity. It does not aim to impose uniformity, far less the hegemony of a dominant culture such as that of Imperial Rome.

Christian theology of the Holy Spirit also undermines any idea of a strict division between the secular and the sacred.

The Spirit is one of the three essential faces or expressions of divinity alongside God the Father and Christ the Son. This subtle concept of a Holy Trinity illuminates how God is both cosmic and personal, defined and numinous, through different kinds of relating. Our divinely created universe is animated by divine presence in complementary ways. The theology of a Spirit-filled creation also explains the interconnections between various faith traditions, even when these may be obscured or as yet undiscovered. All are striving towards the same underlying unity, though in different ways and to varying degrees.

On this understanding, Christianity fosters cultural and political diversity while always measuring their expressions against the unified purposes of the 'kingdom of God'. As a faith tradition that circles the globe, Christianity has no interest in suppressing diversity, despite what some of its advocates have preached and practised in the name of colonial dominance. Cultural identity is not to be subsumed by Christian faith, but affirmed and celebrated as a vital aspect of creation.

Creative interaction in these terms between Scottishness in all its forms and Christianity, or other faith traditions, can be mutually enriching and even defining. Without a cultural context and a distinctive social dynamic to influence, Christianity cannot advance the cause of its kingdom. To impose or dictate such a spiritual vision would be to destroy its own essence, which is freedom, love and justice. Christian faith is a marriage of the sacred and the human, not a forced union, and when functioning at full potential, Christianity should feed cultural diversity and its creative expression. Pentecost gathers nations, peoples and cultures in shared celebration.

As for the Scottish side of the equation, a religious contribution encourages forms of identity that nurture human dignity, self-worth and well-being. Christianity, like other world faiths, challenges inward-looking or prejudicial expressions of culture that do not accord equal respect and dignity to other communities. To affirm self in Christian thinking is to recognize and delight in the identity of others. Diversity thrives as a creative human force if it welcomes mutual respect and influence.

Religion does not claim exclusive ownership of this vision; on the contrary, it affirms it to be part of a common human inheritance, promise and fulfilment.

The concept of diversity in unity and unity in diversity is central to the Pentecost experience. It embraces the nations, peoples, faiths, cultures and languages with a liberating sense of joyful purpose that does not seek to override but to fulfil. Pentecost is in its origins a Harvest Festival and its Christian significance is that Churches are supposed to be about bringing human potential to fruition. This is a direct challenge to Churches that have developed their own diluted forms of culture or pared-down, restricted versions of human life cast in their own institutional moulds.

The aim of Christianity is human freedom and autonomy achieved through love and justice for all. That is the 'kingdom of God' as articulated in words and actions by Christ. This religious narrative is underpinned by faith that all life has a sacred origin and purpose, but that only a freely chosen way of love can realize that inherent promise.

There are no presumptions in Christianity for choosing independent statehood as over against other forms of political order. But there are strong grounds for addressing the distinctiveness of Scotland's environment, society and culture, and for encouraging that society to seek a level of political autonomy that allows all of its citizens to flourish and to make the best possible contribution to our globalized world. It is the job of the Scottish electorate to decide whether those aims are more achievable within the UK or as a fully independent state. This book has set out the ethical and cultural differences between these two options. Either way, the process begun by the re-establishment of the Scottish Parliament is set to continue, because Scotland is already making its own distinctive choices, and there is a need for the political instruments to have the powers to reflect and advance that process.

The part played by religion in either version of a future Scotland will be very different from the past. Existing religious traditions and institutions will either learn the lessons of the dramatic changes that have taken place or fade into obscurity and irrelevance. That, however, would not end religion which is an organic, evolving part of human culture. New expressions of faith would emerge. The emergent Scottish political order will accommodate religion as part of civil society, but will not privilege particular institutions as happened in the past. This process of adjustment will take some time, but the underlying changes that are driving it are already happening.

Richard Holloway, the former Bishop of Edinburgh and Primus of the Scottish Episcopal Church, is a leading critic of the Scottish Churches and their current role in society. His plea is that the new Scotland will be a wholly secular state, and that the contribution of religion should be based on the moral worth of its contribution rather than any presumption of status or influence. The state itself should be tolerant and inclusive, in Holloway's argument, but should not privilege expressions of intolerance or prejudice. Holloway's thinking has been much influenced by the role of most of the Christian Churches in resisting the acceptance of gay people within Scottish society on an equal basis.

This argument is in truth a liberating one for Scottish Christianity, which is trapped within its traditional institutional forms. The power structures of the largest Christian denominations no longer reflect the life of their own communities, far less the wider society. By clinging to outmoded forms of status and top-down governance, they are blocking and not enabling a creative future for Christianity. Removing the external props to these repressive and unresponsive structures would help a different future to happen.

Though such a political change may be described as 'secular', the outcome would not necessarily be further secularization in society or culture. A renewal of religious inspiration on an open and free basis is a possible and positive development, in which a reinvigorated Christianity could play a distinctive part. Although there is much evidence of indifference in Scottish society towards institutional religion, there is also a widespread desire to move beyond the consumer-driven materialism of recent decades. People are on the search for new life choices and these include spiritual alternatives. Socially and politically there is also a sense that top-down strategies for tackling poverty, ill health, addiction and low self-esteem have not worked, and that here too there are cultural and spiritual factors at play that need to be recognized.

Many artists and social thinkers in Scotland have argued that creative freedom is intimately linked with personal and social well-being. For them, spirituality is about that interconnection, rather than some alternative realm disjoined from the material or psychological worlds. In recent decades there has been an increasing sense that these matters are also bound up in our relationship with the natural world. None of these perceptions are foreign to Christianity's source texts, though many of the same artists view the Church as complicit in a social order that has repressed creative autonomy.

Richard Demarco has been a transformational thinker and doer in Scottish culture for over 50 years. He was instrumental in connecting Scotland with a burgeoning international arts scene in the 1960s, but in the 1970s his innovative impetus took a fresh and more reflective turn. He embarked on a series of journeys that were undertaken with groups of artists and activists, and were in themselves a form of creative happenings or explorations. 'The Road to Meikle Seggie' began in Edinburgh's Old Town, moving into its rural environs, into a wider Scotland, and then ranging across Europe. Meikle Seggie was a remote farmsteading on the western flank of the Ochil Hills, which was almost impossible to find and easily missed when one arrived. It was in a sense nowhere and everywhere.

Travelling 'The Road to Meikle Seggie' was about reconnecting the contemporary arts with the environment and with the culture layered through it, that was already the product of generations of human life. But Richard Demarco was also seeking to reshape 'the arts' in a wider non-metropolitan crucible. 'My instinct tells me to make drawings and paintings of the Road to Meikle Seggie,' he writes, and the drawings made on these journeys are a remarkable legacy in their own right. But walking, seeing and drawing also inspired a significant commentary, as Demarco came to feel that these often ancient routes were simultaneously mythic and ordinary:

> I can draw or paint the tangible and observable markers, tracks and trails they leave behind them when they travel in harmony with the Goddess, so my drawings are about what I see in the real world all around me. They are about the magic in all things we recognise as normal. They are not about the paranormal. They are about ordinary roads, and the ordinary things we see on roads – stone walls, farm gates, hedges, telegraph poles, signposts, wayside shrines, trees, grasses, plants, flowers and weeds and how the road moves forward incorporating all of these 'normal' things together with the 'normal' movements of animals and birds, and the wind and the weather they encounter and the movements of clouds and rain storms and shafts of sunlight. They are about ordinary houses and farm buildings, and in the villages and towns they are about paving stones and street corners, drainpipes, gutters, chimney pots, windows, doors, washing hanging out to dry, balconies and all forms of useful street furniture. The road does not concentrate on castles, palaces and cathedrals, or grand and historic buildings. It is governed more by small apparently insignificant details and hidden forces, by underground 'blind' springs and the everchanging movements of shorelines, rivers, and of moonrises and sunsets.

For Richard Demarco the great truth of the myths is that what is exotic and far distant comes to be recognized as what is near at hand, close to home. The marvellous is also the immediate. 'We have failed to learn the truth,' he comments, 'in all the fairy tales we learned on our mothers' laps, that no fairy tale object or event is more exotic or more improbable than the stuff and substance of our everyday lives.'

'The Road to Meikle Seggie' reopens our eyes to the enchantment of the world and to 'the mystery infused in all things'. The Road is Scottish and universal, but passionately grounded in love of the particular. Here Demarco articulates a rooted creative response to the growing environmental crisis, which led to his notable partnership with the German artist Joseph Beuys. A culture disconnected from the sources of life can only be deathly. That insight for Demarco was social and psychological as much as environmental. During this same period he was working inside a Special Unit at Barlinnie Prison in Glasgow with long-term inmates. This brought the art educator's vision into direct contact with the urban poverty of industrialized Scotland, and some of its bleakest human outcomes. A prisoner's perspective on that creative partnership is set out in Jimmy Boyle's 'A Sense of Freedom'.

Richard Demarco set out an agenda in the 1970s for Scottish culture that is visionary and down to earth. He is also pointing to the remaking of religion as the spiritual dynamic of culture. Together they animate a sense of life in all its dimensions that can be creative, connected and sustainable. The artist in every person is a daily expression of the divine. But that artist is also the teacher, the labourer, the child at play, the traveller, the technologist, the philosopher, and the gardener:

> The road leads to a space which reassures the human spirit of its spiritual destiny. It is the space I would like to offer anyone who valued or sought freedom. It is the space I should like to give all those who live and work in prisons where physical journeys are unthinkable.

Since the 1970s Scotland has been on the road to an unknown destination. It has been a journey of almost unimaginable change for those who began in earlier decades, while more readily accepted by those who do not remember a different stateless country. But it is an extraordinary journey, marked most by changes in everyday things, expectations and attitudes. Coffee, tattoos, wind turbines, hardwood saplings, Festivals of everywhere, smokeless pubs, outdoor cafés, female clergy,

MSPs, Enric Miralles's Holyrood. Are we on the 'Road to Meikle Seggie' or just another motorway extension? The only people who can decide that are those who freely choose to live here, and to love everything that this inhabiting does and could mean for Scotland, Europe and the wider world.

# Further Reading

Barker, Margaret, 1996, *The Risen Lord: The Jesus of History as the Christ of Faith*, Edinburgh: T&T Clark.

Bold, Alan, 1988, *MacDiarmid*, London: John Murray.

Borg, Marcus J., 2003, *The Heart of Christianity: Rediscovering a Life of Faith*, New York: HarperCollins.

Boyle, Jimmy, 1977, *Sense of Freedom*, Edinburgh: Canongate Books.

Brown, Callum R., 1997, *Religion and Society in Scotland since 1707*, Edinburgh: Edinburgh University Press.

*Charter for the Arts in Scotland*, 1992, edited by Joyce McMillan, Edinburgh: Scottish Arts Council/COSLA/Scottish Museums Council.

Cheyne, A. C., 1983, *The Transforming of the Kirk: Victorian Scotland's Religious Revolution*, Edinburgh: Saint Andrew Press.

Contributors, 2006, *Religion*, edited by Colin Maclean, and Kenneth Veitch, Scottish Life and Society, Edinburgh: John Donald with EERC and NMS, Vol. 12.

Contributors, 2009, *Growing Citizens: An Interdisciplinary Reflection on Citizenship Education*, edited by Alison Elliot and Heidi Poon, Edinburgh: Saint Andrew Press.

Craig, Cairns, 1999, *The Modern Scottish Novel: Narrative and the National Imagination*, Edinburgh: Edinburgh University Press.

Craig, Carol, 2010, *The Tears that Made the Clyde*, Glendaruel: Argyll Publishing.

Demarco, Richard, 1979, *The Road to Meikle Seggie*, Edinburgh: Richard Demarco Henderson Gallery.

Devine, T. M., 1999, *The Scottish Nation 1700–2000*, London: Allen Lane, Penguin Press.

Fergusson, David, 2004, *Church, State and Civil Society*, Cambridge: Cambridge University Press.

Findlay Bill, Hutchison, David, Scullion, Adrienne, and Smith, Donald, 1998, *A History of Scottish Theatre*, edited by Bill Findlay, Edinburgh: Polygon Press.

Galloway, Janice, 2008, *This is Not About Me*, London: Granta Books.

Gibbon, Lewis Grassic, 1946, *A Scots Quair*, London: Hutchison.

Gray, Alasdair, 2002, *Lanark: A Life in Four Books*, introduced by Janice Galloway, Edinburgh: Canongate Books.

Henderson, Hamish and Contributors, 1980, *The People's Past: Scottish Folk-Scottish History*, edited by Edward Cowan, Edinburgh: Edinburgh University Student Publications Board.

Holloway, Richard, 2013, *A Plea for A Secular Scotland*, Edinburgh: The Saltire Society.

Jenkins, Robin, 1995, *The Changeling*, introduced by Alan Spence, Edinburgh: Canongate Books.

Kesson, Jessie, 1980, *The White Bird Passes*, Edinburgh: Paul Harris Publishing.

Laing, R. D., 1965, *The Divided Self*, London: Penguin Books.

Macdonald, Murdo, 2000, *Scottish Art*, London: Thames and Hudson.

Macmillan, Duncan, 2000, *Scottish Art 1460–2000*, Second Revised Edition, Edinburgh: Mainstream Publishing.

McWhirter, Ian, 2013, *Road to Referendum*, London: Cargo Books.

Maxwell, Stephen, 2012, *Arguing for Independence: Evidence, Risk, and the Wicked Issues*, Edinburgh: Luath Press.

Men, Alexander, 1996, *Christianity or the Twenty-First Century*, edited by Elizabeth Roberts and Ann Shukman, London: SCM Press.

Muir, Edwin, 1954, *An Autobiography*, London: The Hogarth Press.

Nairn, Tom, 1981, *The Break-up of Britain*, Second Expanded Edition, London: Verso.

Petrie, Duncan, 2000, *Screening Scotland*, London: bfi publications.

Robertson, James, 2010, *And the Land Lay Still*, London: Hamish Hamilton.

Scott, P. H., 1979, *The Union of Scotland and England*, Edinburgh: Chambers.

Smith, Donald, 2001, *Storytelling Scotland: A Nation in Narrative*, Edinburgh: Polygon Press.

Smith, Donald, 2009, *God, the Poet and the Devil: Robert Burns and Religion*, Edinburgh: Saint Andrew Press.

Smith, Iain Crichton, 2001, *Consider the Lilies*, introduced by Isobel Murray, Edinburgh: Canongate Books.

Smout, T. C., 1969, *A History of the Scottish People 1560–1830*, Glasgow: Collins.

Stevenson, R. L., 2006, *Kidnapped*, edited by Barry Menikoff, Edinburgh: Canongate Books.

Templeton, Elizabeth, 1991, *God's February: A Life of Archie Craig 1888–1985*, London: BCC/CCBI.

Watson, Roderick, 1995, *The Poetry of Scotland: Gaelic, Scots and English*, Edinburgh: Edinburgh University Press.